50 Greek Island Cuisine Recipes for Home

By: Kelly Johnson

Table of Contents

- Moussaka
- Souvlaki
- Tzatziki
- Spanakopita
- Baklava
- Greek Salad
- Dolmades (Stuffed Grape Leaves)
- Fasolada (Bean Soup)
- Gyro
- Octopus with Oregano
- Pastitsio
- Stifado (Beef Stew)
- Loukoumades (Greek Donuts)
- Kleftiko (Lamb with Garlic)
- Saganaki (Fried Cheese)
- Melitzanosalata (Eggplant Dip)
- Revithosoupa (Chickpea Soup)
- Kalitsounia (Sweet Cheese Pastries)
- Gemista (Stuffed Vegetables)
- Keftedes (Greek Meatballs)
- Galaktoboureko (Custard Pie)
- Patsas (Tripe Soup)
- Koulourakia (Butter Cookies)
- Arni Lemonato (Lamb with Lemon Sauce)
- Horta Vrasta (Boiled Greens)
- Yemista (Stuffed Peppers)
- Psarosoupa (Fish Soup)
- Melomakarona (Honey Cookies)
- Kokoretsi (Offal Dish)
- Briam (Greek Ratatouille)
- Bougatsa (Cream Pie)
- Karidopita (Walnut Cake)
- Papoutsakia (Stuffed Eggplants)
- Garides Saganaki (Shrimp in Tomato Sauce)
- Strapatsada (Scrambled Eggs with Tomato and Feta)
- Tyropita (Cheese Pie)

- Kolokithokeftedes (Zucchini Fritters)
- Pitarakia (Sweet Fried Dough)
- Marides Tiganites (Fried Anchovies)
- Dakos (Barley Rusk Salad)
- Pitaroudia (Chickpea Fritters)
- Soutzoukakia (Meatballs in Tomato Sauce)
- Lazarakia (Lenten Cookies)
- Anginares a la Polita (Artichokes with Lemon and Olive Oil)
- Pasteli (Sesame Seed and Honey Bars)
- Imam Baildi (Stuffed Eggplant)
- Karithopita (Walnut Cake)
- Fakes Soupa (Lentil Soup)
- Psomi (Greek Bread)
- Loukaniko (Greek Sausage)

Moussaka

Ingredients:

For the Moussaka Layers:

- 2-3 large eggplants (aubergines), sliced lengthwise into 1/4 inch thick slices
- Salt
- Olive oil for brushing and frying
- 1 large onion, finely chopped
- 2-3 garlic cloves, minced
- 1 lb (500g) ground lamb or beef
- 1 can (14 oz/400g) diced tomatoes
- 1/2 cup red wine (optional)
- 1 tsp dried oregano
- 1/2 tsp ground cinnamon
- Salt and pepper to taste

For the Béchamel Sauce:

- 4 tbsp unsalted butter
- 1/4 cup all-purpose flour
- 2 cups milk
- Pinch of nutmeg
- Salt and pepper to taste
- 1/2 cup grated Parmesan cheese (optional)

Instructions:

1. **Prepare the Eggplant:**
   - Sprinkle the eggplant slices with salt and let them sit for about 30 minutes to draw out bitterness. Rinse and pat dry with paper towels.
   - Brush both sides of the eggplant slices with olive oil and grill or fry them in batches until golden brown. Set aside on paper towels to drain excess oil.
2. **Prepare the Meat Sauce:**
   - In a large skillet or pan, heat some olive oil over medium heat. Add the chopped onion and sauté until softened.
   - Add the minced garlic and cook for another minute until fragrant.
   - Add the ground lamb or beef, breaking it up with a spoon, and cook until browned.
   - Stir in the diced tomatoes, red wine (if using), oregano, cinnamon, salt, and pepper. Simmer for about 20-30 minutes until the sauce has thickened. Remove from heat and set aside.
3. **Make the Béchamel Sauce:**

- In a saucepan, melt the butter over medium heat. Once melted, add the flour and whisk continuously for about 1-2 minutes until it forms a smooth paste (roux).
- Gradually whisk in the milk, a little at a time, until smooth and thickened.
- Add a pinch of nutmeg and season with salt and pepper to taste. Stir in grated Parmesan cheese if using. Remove from heat and set aside.

4. **Assemble the Moussaka:**
    - Preheat the oven to 375°F (190°C).
    - Arrange half of the eggplant slices in a layer in a greased baking dish (about 9x13 inches).
    - Spread half of the meat sauce over the eggplant layer.
    - Arrange the remaining eggplant slices on top of the meat sauce.
    - Spread the remaining meat sauce evenly over the eggplant.
    - Pour the béchamel sauce over the top, spreading it evenly with a spatula to cover the entire surface.

5. **Bake the Moussaka:**
    - Place the baking dish in the preheated oven and bake for 45-50 minutes, or until the top is golden brown and bubbly.
    - Remove from the oven and let it cool for about 15 minutes before serving.

6. **Serve:**
    - Moussaka is traditionally served warm. Cut into squares or rectangles and serve with a Greek salad and crusty bread.

Enjoy this rich and flavorful Greek dish, perfect for showcasing the delicious flavors of the Mediterranean!

Souvlaki

Ingredients:

For the Souvlaki Marinade:

- 1.5 lbs (700g) of pork shoulder or chicken breast, cut into 1-inch cubes
- 1/4 cup olive oil
- Juice of 1 lemon
- 3 garlic cloves, minced
- 1 tsp dried oregano
- 1/2 tsp dried thyme
- 1/2 tsp dried rosemary
- Salt and pepper to taste

For Serving:

- Pita bread
- Tzatziki sauce (see recipe below)
- Sliced tomatoes
- Sliced red onions
- Chopped fresh parsley
- Lemon wedges

Instructions:

1. **Prepare the Marinade:**
    - In a bowl, combine olive oil, lemon juice, minced garlic, dried oregano, thyme, rosemary, salt, and pepper. Mix well.
2. **Marinate the Meat:**
    - Place the cubed meat in a shallow dish or resealable plastic bag. Pour the marinade over the meat and toss to coat evenly. Cover the dish or seal the bag and refrigerate for at least 1 hour, preferably longer (up to 4 hours), to allow the flavors to meld.
3. **Prepare the Tzatziki Sauce:**
    - Tzatziki is a classic Greek sauce made with yogurt, cucumber, garlic, olive oil, and herbs. Here's a simple recipe:
        - 1 cup Greek yogurt
        - 1/2 cucumber, grated and squeezed to remove excess moisture
        - 2 cloves garlic, minced
        - 1 tbsp olive oil
        - 1 tbsp lemon juice
        - 1 tbsp chopped fresh dill (or 1 tsp dried dill)
        - Salt and pepper to taste

- Mix all ingredients in a bowl until well combined. Adjust seasoning to taste. Refrigerate until ready to serve.

4. **Skewer and Grill the Souvlaki:**
   - Preheat the grill to medium-high heat.
   - Thread the marinated meat onto skewers. If using wooden skewers, soak them in water for at least 30 minutes before threading to prevent burning.
   - Grill the skewers for about 10-12 minutes, turning occasionally, until the meat is cooked through and slightly charred on the edges.
5. **Serve the Souvlaki:**
   - Warm the pita bread on the grill for a minute or so on each side.
   - Serve the souvlaki skewers hot with warm pita bread, tzatziki sauce, sliced tomatoes, sliced red onions, chopped fresh parsley, and lemon wedges on the side.
6. **Enjoy:**
   - To eat, place some souvlaki meat inside a piece of pita bread, add tzatziki sauce, and your desired toppings. Roll it up and enjoy this delicious and flavorful Greek street food!

Souvlaki is perfect for a casual meal or outdoor barbecue, bringing the authentic flavors of Greece right to your table.

Tzatziki

Ingredients:

- 1 cup Greek yogurt (plain, full-fat)
- 1/2 cucumber, grated and excess moisture squeezed out
- 2 cloves garlic, minced
- 1 tbsp extra virgin olive oil
- 1 tbsp lemon juice (about half a lemon)
- 1 tbsp chopped fresh dill (or 1 tsp dried dill)
- Salt and pepper, to taste

Instructions:

1. **Prepare the Cucumber:**
   - Grate the cucumber using a box grater. Place the grated cucumber in a clean kitchen towel or cheesecloth and squeeze out as much liquid as possible. Alternatively, you can use a fine mesh sieve and press down with a spoon to extract the moisture.
2. **Mix Ingredients:**
   - In a medium bowl, combine the Greek yogurt, grated cucumber, minced garlic, olive oil, lemon juice, and chopped dill. Mix well to combine.
3. **Season:**
   - Season the tzatziki with salt and pepper to taste. Adjust the amount of garlic, lemon juice, or dill according to your preference.
4. **Chill:**
   - Cover the bowl with plastic wrap or transfer the tzatziki to an airtight container. Refrigerate for at least 1 hour to allow the flavors to meld together.
5. **Serve:**
   - Stir the tzatziki before serving. You can garnish with a drizzle of olive oil and a sprig of fresh dill if desired.
   - Serve tzatziki as a dip with pita bread, vegetable sticks, or alongside grilled meats like souvlaki or gyros.

Enjoy this homemade tzatziki sauce that's creamy, tangy, and full of Mediterranean flavors! Adjust the ingredients to suit your taste preferences and use it to complement a variety of dishes or as a refreshing dip.

Spanakopita

Ingredients:

- 1 package (about 1 lb) phyllo dough, thawed if frozen
- 1/2 cup unsalted butter, melted
- 1 lb fresh spinach, washed and chopped (or 2 packages frozen spinach, thawed and squeezed dry)
- 1 bunch green onions, finely chopped
- 1 small onion, finely chopped
- 2 cloves garlic, minced
- 1/2 cup fresh dill, chopped (or 2 tbsp dried dill)
- 1/2 cup fresh parsley, chopped
- 8 oz feta cheese, crumbled
- 1 cup ricotta cheese (or cottage cheese)
- 3 eggs, lightly beaten
- Salt and pepper, to taste
- Olive oil for brushing

Instructions:

1. **Prepare the Filling:**
   - If using fresh spinach, wash and chop it. If using frozen spinach, thaw it completely and squeeze out as much moisture as possible using a clean kitchen towel.
   - In a large skillet or frying pan, heat some olive oil over medium heat. Add the chopped onions and garlic, and sauté until softened and translucent, about 5 minutes.
   - Add the spinach in batches (if using fresh) and cook until wilted. If using frozen spinach, add it to the skillet and cook for a few minutes until heated through.
   - Remove from heat and let the spinach mixture cool slightly. Transfer to a large bowl.
2. **Prepare the Cheese Mixture:**
   - To the bowl with the spinach, add the chopped green onions, dill, parsley, crumbled feta cheese, ricotta cheese, and beaten eggs. Season with salt and pepper to taste. Mix everything together until well combined.
3. **Assemble the Spanakopita:**
   - Preheat the oven to 375°F (190°C). Grease a baking dish (about 9x13 inches) with olive oil or butter.
   - Unroll the phyllo dough and cover it with a damp kitchen towel to prevent it from drying out.
   - Brush the bottom of the baking dish with melted butter.

- Place one sheet of phyllo dough in the baking dish and brush it with melted butter. Repeat with 7-8 more sheets, layering each sheet and brushing with butter.
- Spread the spinach and cheese mixture evenly over the phyllo dough in the baking dish.

4. **Layer the Phyllo Dough:**
   - Cover the spinach mixture with another sheet of phyllo dough and brush with melted butter. Repeat with 7-8 more sheets, brushing each sheet with butter.
   - After the final layer of phyllo dough, tuck any overhanging edges into the sides of the baking dish to create a neat edge.

5. **Bake the Spanakopita:**
   - Using a sharp knife, score the top layers of phyllo dough into squares or diamonds (this will make it easier to cut after baking).
   - Bake in the preheated oven for 45-55 minutes, or until the top is golden brown and crispy.

6. **Serve:**
   - Remove from the oven and let it cool for a few minutes before slicing and serving. Spanakopita is delicious served warm or at room temperature.

Spanakopita is a delightful dish that showcases the flavors of spinach and feta cheese wrapped in layers of crispy phyllo dough. It's perfect for parties, gatherings, or as a special treat any time of the year!

Baklava

Ingredients:

For the Baklava:

- 1 package (about 1 lb) phyllo dough, thawed if frozen
- 1 cup unsalted butter, melted
- 2 cups mixed nuts (such as walnuts, pistachios, and almonds), finely chopped
- 1/2 cup granulated sugar
- 1 tsp ground cinnamon
- 1/4 tsp ground cloves (optional)

For the Syrup:

- 1 cup water
- 1 cup granulated sugar
- 1/2 cup honey
- 1 cinnamon stick
- 3-4 whole cloves (optional)
- 1 tbsp lemon juice

Instructions:

1. **Prepare the Nut Filling:**
   - In a bowl, combine the chopped nuts, sugar, cinnamon, and ground cloves (if using). Mix well and set aside.
2. **Prepare the Phyllo Dough:**
   - Preheat the oven to 350°F (175°C). Grease a baking dish (about 9x13 inches) with melted butter.
   - Unroll the phyllo dough and cover it with a damp kitchen towel to prevent it from drying out while you work.
3. **Assemble the Baklava:**
   - Place one sheet of phyllo dough in the bottom of the greased baking dish. Brush it generously with melted butter.
   - Repeat the layering process, placing one sheet of phyllo dough at a time and brushing each sheet with melted butter, until you have used about half of the phyllo dough sheets.
4. **Add the Nut Filling:**
   - Sprinkle about 1/3 of the nut mixture evenly over the layered phyllo dough.
5. **Continue Layering:**
   - Continue layering the remaining phyllo dough sheets one at a time, brushing each sheet with melted butter.
   - After placing about half of the remaining phyllo sheets, sprinkle another 1/3 of the nut mixture over the layers.

- Continue layering the rest of the phyllo sheets, brushing each with butter, until you have used all of the phyllo dough sheets.
6. **Cut the Baklava:**
   - Using a sharp knife, carefully cut the baklava into diamond or square shapes. Make sure to cut all the way through the layers.
7. **Bake the Baklava:**
   - Place the baking dish in the preheated oven and bake for 45-50 minutes, or until the baklava is golden brown and crisp.
8. **Prepare the Syrup:**
   - While the baklava is baking, make the syrup. In a saucepan, combine water, sugar, honey, cinnamon stick, and whole cloves (if using).
   - Bring the mixture to a boil, then reduce the heat and simmer for about 10-15 minutes, stirring occasionally, until the syrup slightly thickens.
   - Remove from heat and stir in the lemon juice. Let the syrup cool slightly.
9. **Pour the Syrup:**
   - Once the baklava is done baking and while it is still hot, carefully pour the cooled syrup evenly over the hot baklava. Make sure to cover all the cuts and edges.
10. **Let it Cool:**
- Allow the baklava to cool completely in the pan, absorbing the syrup.
11. **Serve:**
- Once cooled, carefully lift out the pieces and arrange them on a serving platter. Baklava is typically served at room temperature.

Enjoy this delicious and sweet treat that combines crispy layers of phyllo dough with a nutty filling and aromatic syrup! Baklava is perfect for special occasions or any time you want to indulge in a delightful dessert with Mediterranean flair.

Greek Salad

Ingredients:

- 4 medium tomatoes, cut into wedges or chunks
- 1 cucumber, sliced into rounds or chunks
- 1 green bell pepper, seeded and sliced
- 1 red onion, thinly sliced
- 1/2 cup Kalamata olives, pitted
- 1/2 cup feta cheese, crumbled
- Fresh oregano leaves (optional), for garnish

For the Dressing:

- 1/4 cup extra virgin olive oil
- 2 tbsp red wine vinegar or lemon juice
- 1-2 cloves garlic, minced
- 1 tsp dried oregano
- Salt and freshly ground black pepper, to taste

Instructions:

1. **Prepare the Vegetables:**
   - In a large salad bowl, combine the tomato wedges, cucumber slices, green bell pepper slices, and thinly sliced red onion.
2. **Add the Olives and Feta:**
   - Add the Kalamata olives and crumbled feta cheese to the bowl with the vegetables.
3. **Make the Dressing:**
   - In a small bowl or jar, whisk together the extra virgin olive oil, red wine vinegar (or lemon juice), minced garlic, dried oregano, salt, and pepper until well combined.
4. **Assemble the Salad:**
   - Drizzle the dressing over the salad ingredients in the bowl.
5. **Toss Gently:**
   - Gently toss the salad with clean hands or salad tongs to coat the vegetables evenly with the dressing.
6. **Garnish and Serve:**
   - Garnish the Greek salad with fresh oregano leaves if desired.
   - Serve immediately as a side dish or as a light main course with crusty bread.

Tips:

- **Variations:** You can add other ingredients like cherry tomatoes, capers, or even a sprinkle of dried chili flakes for a spicy kick.

- **Storage:** Greek salad is best enjoyed fresh, but you can store leftovers in an airtight container in the refrigerator for up to 1 day. The flavors may intensify as it sits.
- **Serve Chilled:** For the best taste, chill the salad in the refrigerator for about 30 minutes before serving to allow the flavors to meld together.

This Greek Salad recipe captures the essence of Mediterranean cuisine with its bright colors, fresh ingredients, and tangy dressing. It's a perfect addition to any meal or a refreshing dish on its own during warm weather.

Dolmades (Stuffed Grape Leaves)

Ingredients:

For the Dolmades:

- 1 jar (about 60-70) grape leaves in brine, rinsed and drained
- 1 cup short-grain white rice
- 1/2 lb ground lamb or beef (optional)
- 1/2 cup finely chopped onion
- 1/4 cup pine nuts (optional)
- 1/4 cup chopped fresh dill
- 1/4 cup chopped fresh mint
- 1/4 cup chopped fresh parsley
- 1/4 cup extra virgin olive oil
- Juice of 1-2 lemons
- Salt and freshly ground black pepper, to taste

For Cooking:

- Water
- 1-2 lemons, sliced
- Extra virgin olive oil

Instructions:

1. **Prepare the Grape Leaves:**
   - Rinse the grape leaves thoroughly under cold water to remove excess brine. If using jarred grape leaves, gently separate them and place them in a bowl of warm water to soften while you prepare the filling.
2. **Prepare the Filling:**
   - In a large bowl, combine the rice, ground lamb or beef (if using), chopped onion, pine nuts (if using), chopped dill, mint, parsley, olive oil, lemon juice, salt, and pepper. Mix well until all ingredients are evenly incorporated.
3. **Assemble the Dolmades:**
   - Lay a grape leaf flat on a clean surface, vein-side up, with the stem end facing you. Place a tablespoon of the rice filling near the stem end of the leaf.
   - Fold the stem end over the filling, then fold in the sides, and roll tightly to form a compact cylinder. Repeat with the remaining grape leaves and filling.
4. **Cook the Dolmades:**
   - Line the bottom of a large pot with a few grape leaves (this prevents the dolmades from sticking to the pot).
   - Arrange the dolmades in the pot, seam side down, in tight layers. Place lemon slices between the layers and drizzle with olive oil.

- Pour enough water into the pot to just cover the dolmades. Place a plate or a lid that fits inside the pot over the dolmades to keep them from unraveling during cooking.
5. **Simmer the Dolmades:**
    - Bring the water to a boil over medium-high heat. Reduce the heat to low, cover the pot, and simmer gently for 45-60 minutes, or until the rice is fully cooked and the grape leaves are tender.
6. **Serve:**
    - Remove the dolmades from the pot using a slotted spoon and arrange them on a serving platter.
    - Serve dolmades warm or at room temperature. They are delicious on their own or with a dollop of tzatziki sauce.

Tips:

- **Storage:** Dolmades can be stored in an airtight container in the refrigerator for up to 3 days. They can be enjoyed cold or gently reheated before serving.
- **Variations:** You can customize the filling by adding currants, pine nuts, or adjusting the herbs to suit your taste preferences.
- **Vegetarian Option:** To make vegetarian dolmades, simply omit the ground meat and increase the amount of rice in the filling.

Dolmades are a delightful appetizer or side dish that showcases the flavors of fresh herbs and tender grape leaves. They are a labor of love but well worth the effort for their delicious taste and cultural significance in Greek cuisine.

Fasolada (Bean Soup)

Ingredients:

- 1 cup dried white beans (such as navy beans or great northern beans), soaked overnight
- 1/4 cup extra virgin olive oil
- 1 large onion, finely chopped
- 2-3 carrots, peeled and diced
- 2-3 celery stalks, diced
- 4 cloves garlic, minced
- 1 can (14 oz) diced tomatoes
- 1 tbsp tomato paste
- 1 bay leaf
- 1 tsp dried oregano
- Salt and freshly ground black pepper, to taste
- Juice of 1 lemon (optional)
- Fresh parsley, chopped, for garnish

Instructions:

1. **Prepare the Beans:**
   - Rinse the dried beans under cold water and soak them in a large bowl with enough water to cover them by a few inches. Let them soak overnight (or for at least 8 hours). Drain and rinse the beans before cooking.
2. **Cook the Soup:**
   - In a large pot or Dutch oven, heat the olive oil over medium heat. Add the chopped onion, carrots, and celery. Sauté for about 5-7 minutes until the vegetables start to soften.
3. **Add Garlic and Tomatoes:**
   - Add the minced garlic to the pot and sauté for another minute until fragrant.
   - Stir in the diced tomatoes, tomato paste, bay leaf, and dried oregano. Cook for a few minutes, stirring occasionally.
4. **Simmer the Soup:**
   - Add the soaked and drained beans to the pot. Pour in enough water to cover the beans and vegetables by about 2 inches.
   - Bring the soup to a boil over medium-high heat. Reduce the heat to low, cover the pot, and simmer gently for about 1.5 to 2 hours, or until the beans are tender and cooked through. Stir occasionally and add more water if needed to keep the beans covered.
5. **Season and Serve:**
   - Once the beans are tender, season the soup with salt and pepper to taste. If desired, add a squeeze of fresh lemon juice for brightness.
   - Remove the bay leaf from the soup.
6. **Serve:**

- Ladle the Fasolada into bowls and garnish with chopped fresh parsley.
- Serve hot, optionally accompanied by crusty bread or a side of Greek salad.

Tips:

- **Variations:** Some variations of Fasolada include adding potatoes, spinach, or other greens. You can also adjust the consistency by blending a portion of the soup to make it creamier.
- **Storage:** Fasolada tastes even better the next day as the flavors develop. Store leftovers in an airtight container in the refrigerator for up to 4-5 days, or freeze for longer storage.
- **Tradition:** Fasolada is often served as a main course in Greece, accompanied by olives, feta cheese, and bread.

This Greek bean soup is not only delicious and comforting but also nutritious and filling, making it a perfect dish for any occasion, especially when you want to enjoy a taste of traditional Greek cuisine.

Gyro

Ingredients:

For the Gyro Meat:

- 1 lb (450g) boneless pork shoulder, chicken breast, or lamb leg, thinly sliced
- 2 tbsp extra virgin olive oil
- Juice of 1 lemon
- 3 cloves garlic, minced
- 1 tsp dried oregano
- 1 tsp paprika
- 1/2 tsp ground cumin
- 1/2 tsp ground coriander
- Salt and pepper, to taste

For Serving:

- Pita bread
- Sliced tomatoes
- Sliced red onions
- Sliced cucumbers
- Tzatziki sauce (see recipe in previous responses)
- French fries (optional)

Instructions:

1. **Prepare the Gyro Meat:**
   - In a bowl, combine the olive oil, lemon juice, minced garlic, dried oregano, paprika, ground cumin, ground coriander, salt, and pepper. Mix well.
   - Add the thinly sliced meat to the marinade and toss until the meat is evenly coated. Cover the bowl and refrigerate for at least 1 hour, or ideally overnight, to marinate.
2. **Cook the Gyro Meat:**
   - Heat a large skillet or grill pan over medium-high heat.
   - Add the marinated meat slices to the hot skillet in a single layer. Cook for about 3-4 minutes on each side, or until the meat is cooked through and lightly browned. You may need to cook the meat in batches to avoid overcrowding the pan.
   - Remove the cooked meat from the skillet and let it rest for a few minutes before slicing it thinly.
3. **Assemble the Gyro Sandwich:**
   - Warm the pita bread briefly in a toaster oven, oven, or microwave.
   - Spread a generous amount of tzatziki sauce on the inside of the pita bread.

- Layer the sliced gyro meat, sliced tomatoes, sliced red onions, and sliced cucumbers inside the pita.
- Optionally, add French fries inside the pita for extra crunch and flavor.
4. **Serve:**
    - Fold the pita bread over the filling to form a sandwich.
    - Serve the gyro sandwich immediately, optionally with extra tzatziki sauce on the side and a side of Greek salad.

Tips:

- **Variations:** You can customize your gyro with different meats or additional toppings like lettuce, feta cheese, or pickled peppers.
- **Grilling Option:** If you have access to a vertical rotisserie (traditional for making gyros), you can stack the marinated meat slices on the rotisserie skewer and cook them slowly until crispy and cooked through.
- **Leftovers:** Gyro meat and assembled sandwiches can be stored in the refrigerator. Reheat the meat gently in a skillet or microwave before serving.

Enjoy this homemade gyro sandwich filled with tender, flavorful meat, fresh vegetables, and creamy tzatziki sauce. It's a delicious taste of Greece that's perfect for a casual meal or gathering with friends and family!

Octopus with Oregano

Ingredients:

- 1 large octopus (about 2-3 lbs), cleaned and thawed if frozen
- 1/2 cup extra virgin olive oil
- Juice of 1-2 lemons
- 4-5 garlic cloves, minced
- 2 tbsp dried oregano (or 1/4 cup chopped fresh oregano)
- Salt and freshly ground black pepper, to taste
- Lemon wedges, for serving

Instructions:

1. **Prepare the Octopus:**
    - If using fresh octopus, clean it thoroughly by removing the beak, eyes, and intestines. Rinse under cold water.
    - If using frozen octopus, thaw it in the refrigerator overnight before cooking.
2. **Tenderize the Octopus:**
    - To tenderize the octopus, you can either:
        - Beat it against a hard surface (such as a sink) for several minutes.
        - Freeze and thaw it a couple of times before cooking.
        - Slow cook it in water for about an hour before grilling or frying.
3. **Marinate the Octopus:**
    - In a large bowl, whisk together the olive oil, lemon juice, minced garlic, dried oregano (if using fresh oregano, add it later), salt, and pepper.
    - Add the octopus to the marinade and toss to coat evenly. Cover the bowl and refrigerate for at least 1 hour, or up to overnight, to allow the flavors to meld.
4. **Cook the Octopus:**
    - Preheat the grill to medium-high heat or prepare a grill pan on the stove over medium-high heat.
    - Remove the octopus from the marinade and grill it for about 3-4 minutes per side, or until it is lightly charred and cooked through. Alternatively, you can roast it in the oven at 400°F (200°C) for about 20-25 minutes, or until tender.
    - If using fresh oregano, sprinkle it over the octopus during the last few minutes of cooking.
5. **Serve:**
    - Transfer the grilled octopus to a serving platter.
    - Serve hot, garnished with lemon wedges for squeezing over the octopus.

Tips:

- **Tenderizing:** Octopus can be tough, so tenderizing it before cooking helps to achieve a more tender texture.

- **Grilling:** Grilling gives octopus a delicious smoky flavor, but you can also boil it before grilling to ensure tenderness.
- **Serving:** Octopus with oregano is often served as a main dish with a side of Greek salad, crusty bread, or potatoes.

This dish is simple yet flavorful, allowing the natural taste of the octopus to shine through while enhancing it with the brightness of lemon and the earthiness of oregano. It's a delightful addition to any Mediterranean-inspired meal!

Pastitsio

Ingredients:

For the Meat Sauce:

- 1 lb ground beef or lamb
- 1 onion, finely chopped
- 3 cloves garlic, minced
- 1 can (14 oz) diced tomatoes
- 1/2 cup tomato sauce or tomato paste
- 1/2 cup red wine (optional)
- 1 tsp dried oregano
- 1/2 tsp ground cinnamon
- Salt and freshly ground black pepper, to taste
- 2 tbsp extra virgin olive oil

For the Pasta:

- 1 lb penne or ziti pasta (or any tubular pasta), cooked al dente according to package instructions
- 1/4 cup grated Parmesan cheese
- 2 tbsp butter

For the Béchamel Sauce:

- 1/2 cup unsalted butter
- 1/2 cup all-purpose flour
- 4 cups milk, warmed
- 1/4 tsp ground nutmeg
- Salt and freshly ground black pepper, to taste
- 2 eggs
- 1/2 cup grated Parmesan cheese

Instructions:

1. **Prepare the Meat Sauce:**
   - In a large skillet or frying pan, heat the olive oil over medium-high heat. Add the chopped onion and sauté until softened, about 5 minutes.
   - Add the minced garlic and cook for another minute until fragrant.
   - Add the ground beef or lamb to the skillet, breaking it up with a spoon. Cook until browned and cooked through.
   - Stir in the diced tomatoes, tomato sauce or paste, red wine (if using), dried oregano, ground cinnamon, salt, and pepper. Simmer the sauce for about 20-30 minutes, stirring occasionally, until thickened. Remove from heat and set aside.

2. **Cook the Pasta:**
   - Cook the penne or ziti pasta in a large pot of salted boiling water until al dente according to the package instructions. Drain the pasta and return it to the pot.
   - Stir in the grated Parmesan cheese and butter until the pasta is evenly coated. Set aside.
3. **Prepare the Béchamel Sauce:**
   - In a large saucepan, melt the butter over medium heat. Once melted, whisk in the flour to form a paste (roux). Cook the roux for 1-2 minutes, stirring constantly.
   - Gradually whisk in the warm milk, a little at a time, until smooth and creamy. Cook the sauce, stirring constantly, until it thickens and comes to a simmer.
   - Stir in the ground nutmeg, salt, and pepper to taste. Remove the saucepan from the heat and let it cool slightly.
   - In a small bowl, lightly beat the eggs. Gradually whisk the beaten eggs into the warm béchamel sauce until well combined. Stir in the grated Parmesan cheese.
4. **Assemble the Pastitsio:**
   - Preheat the oven to 350°F (175°C). Grease a large baking dish (about 9x13 inches) with butter or cooking spray.
   - Spread half of the cooked pasta evenly on the bottom of the prepared baking dish.
   - Spread the meat sauce evenly over the pasta layer.
   - Top the meat sauce with the remaining pasta, spreading it evenly.
   - Pour the béchamel sauce over the top layer of pasta, spreading it evenly with a spatula.
5. **Bake the Pastitsio:**
   - Place the baking dish in the preheated oven and bake for about 45-55 minutes, or until the top is golden brown and bubbly.
   - Remove from the oven and let it cool for about 10-15 minutes before slicing and serving.
6. **Serve:**
   - Slice the Pastitsio into squares and serve warm. It pairs wonderfully with a Greek salad and crusty bread.

Tips:

- **Make-Ahead:** Pastitsio can be assembled ahead of time and refrigerated (unbaked) for up to 1 day before baking. Bring it to room temperature before baking.
- **Leftovers:** Store leftover Pastitsio in an airtight container in the refrigerator for up to 3-4 days. Reheat in the oven or microwave until warmed through.

This delicious and comforting Greek dish combines layers of pasta, savory meat sauce, and creamy béchamel sauce for a satisfying meal that's perfect for gatherings or family dinners. Enjoy the rich flavors and hearty textures of homemade Pastitsio!

Stifado (Beef Stew)

Ingredients:

- 2 lbs stewing beef (such as chuck), cut into chunks
- 4-5 tbsp extra virgin olive oil
- 4-5 medium onions, thinly sliced
- 4 cloves garlic, minced
- 2 tbsp tomato paste
- 1 cup red wine
- 1 can (14 oz) diced tomatoes
- 1 cup beef broth
- 2 bay leaves
- 1 cinnamon stick
- 1 tsp dried oregano
- 1/2 tsp ground cloves
- Salt and freshly ground black pepper, to taste
- 1 tbsp red wine vinegar (optional, for a touch of acidity)
- Chopped fresh parsley, for garnish

Instructions:

1. **Brown the Beef:**
    - In a large Dutch oven or heavy-bottomed pot, heat 2 tablespoons of olive oil over medium-high heat.
    - Pat the beef chunks dry with paper towels and season generously with salt and pepper.
    - Working in batches, brown the beef on all sides until deeply caramelized. Transfer the browned beef to a plate and set aside.
2. **Cook the Onions:**
    - In the same pot, add the remaining olive oil if needed. Add the sliced onions and cook over medium heat until softened and golden brown, about 10-12 minutes.
    - Add the minced garlic and cook for another minute until fragrant.
3. **Combine Ingredients:**
    - Stir in the tomato paste and cook for 1-2 minutes to deepen the flavors.
    - Deglaze the pot with the red wine, scraping up any browned bits from the bottom.
    - Add the diced tomatoes (with their juices), beef broth, bay leaves, cinnamon stick, dried oregano, and ground cloves. Stir to combine.
4. **Simmer the Stew:**
    - Return the browned beef to the pot, along with any accumulated juices. Bring the mixture to a simmer.
    - Reduce the heat to low, cover the pot with a lid slightly ajar, and simmer gently for 2-2.5 hours, stirring occasionally, or until the beef is tender and the sauce has

thickened. Add more beef broth or water if needed to maintain a stew-like consistency.
5. **Finish the Stifado:**
    - Taste and adjust seasoning with salt and pepper as needed. If desired, add a tablespoon of red wine vinegar for a touch of acidity.
    - Remove the bay leaves and cinnamon stick before serving.
6. **Serve:**
    - Ladle the Stifado into bowls and garnish with chopped fresh parsley.
    - Serve hot, accompanied by crusty bread, rice, or mashed potatoes.

Tips:

- **Variations:** Some variations of Stifado include adding pearl onions or mushrooms for added depth of flavor.
- **Make-Ahead:** Stifado tastes even better the next day as the flavors meld together. It can be stored in the refrigerator for up to 3-4 days or frozen for longer storage.
- **Storing Leftovers:** Store leftovers in an airtight container in the refrigerator and reheat gently on the stove or in the microwave.

This Greek beef stew is comforting, aromatic, and perfect for a cozy meal with family and friends. Enjoy the rich flavors of Stifado served alongside your favorite sides for a satisfying dining experience.

Loukoumades (Greek Donuts)

Ingredients:

For the Loukoumades:

- 1 cup lukewarm water
- 1 tsp active dry yeast
- 1 tbsp granulated sugar
- 2 cups all-purpose flour
- 1/4 tsp salt
- Vegetable oil, for frying

For the Syrup:

- 1/2 cup honey
- 1/2 cup water
- 1 cinnamon stick (optional)
- 1 strip of lemon zest (optional)
- Chopped nuts (such as walnuts or almonds), for garnish (optional)
- Ground cinnamon, for sprinkling

Instructions:

1. **Prepare the Dough:**
    - In a large mixing bowl, combine the lukewarm water, active dry yeast, and granulated sugar. Let it sit for about 5-10 minutes until the yeast activates and becomes frothy.
2. **Make the Batter:**
    - Stir in the flour and salt gradually, mixing until smooth. The batter should be thick and sticky, similar to pancake batter consistency.
    - Cover the bowl with a clean kitchen towel and let the batter rest in a warm place for about 1-2 hours, or until it doubles in size and becomes bubbly.
3. **Heat the Oil:**
    - In a deep pot or Dutch oven, heat enough vegetable oil to submerge the loukoumades (about 2-3 inches) to 350°F (175°C) over medium heat.
4. **Fry the Loukoumades:**
    - Once the oil is hot, use two spoons or a small ice cream scoop to carefully drop spoonfuls of batter into the hot oil, shaping them into small rounds (about 1-2 inches in diameter). You can fry about 4-5 loukoumades at a time, depending on the size of your pot.
    - Fry the loukoumades for 2-3 minutes on each side, or until they are golden brown and puffed up. Use a slotted spoon to remove them from the oil and transfer them to a plate lined with paper towels to drain excess oil.
5. **Make the Syrup:**

- In a small saucepan, combine the honey, water, cinnamon stick, and lemon zest (if using). Bring the mixture to a simmer over medium heat, stirring occasionally.
- Let the syrup simmer for about 5 minutes until slightly thickened. Remove from heat and discard the cinnamon stick and lemon zest.

6. **Serve:**
   - Arrange the fried loukoumades on a serving platter. Drizzle the warm honey syrup over the loukoumades.
   - Sprinkle chopped nuts (if using) and ground cinnamon over the top.
   - Serve the loukoumades warm and enjoy them immediately.

Tips:

- **Temperature Control:** Maintain the oil temperature around 350°F (175°C) for even frying and crispy loukoumades.
- **Flavor Variations:** Some variations include adding orange zest or a pinch of ground cloves to the batter for extra flavor.
- **Storage:** Loukoumades are best enjoyed fresh but can be stored in an airtight container at room temperature for up to 1 day. Reheat briefly in the oven before serving if desired.

Loukoumades are a delightful treat that brings the flavors of Greece into your home. Enjoy these crispy, fluffy donuts coated in honey syrup and aromatic spices for a taste of Greek tradition!

Kleftiko (Lamb with Garlic)

Ingredients:

- 1.5 kg (3.3 lbs) lamb shoulder or leg, cut into large chunks
- 6-8 garlic cloves, sliced
- Juice of 2 lemons
- 4 tbsp olive oil
- 1 tbsp dried oregano
- Salt and pepper to taste
- 2-3 large potatoes, peeled and cut into wedges (optional)
- 1 onion, sliced (optional)
- 1 cup chicken or lamb stock (optional)

Instructions:

1. **Marinate the Lamb:**
    - Place the lamb pieces in a large bowl.
    - Add the sliced garlic, lemon juice, olive oil, dried oregano, salt, and pepper.
    - Mix well to coat the lamb evenly.
    - Cover the bowl with plastic wrap and marinate in the refrigerator for at least 2 hours, or preferably overnight for the flavors to meld.
2. **Preheat the Oven:**
    - Preheat your oven to 160°C (320°F) for fan ovens, or 180°C (355°F) for conventional ovens.
3. **Prepare the Dish:**
    - If using potatoes and onions, spread them evenly on the bottom of a large baking dish to create a bed for the lamb. This will help elevate the lamb while cooking and add flavor to the vegetables.
4. **Cooking:**
    - Place the marinated lamb on top of the potatoes and onions, or directly into the baking dish if not using vegetables.
    - Pour the marinade over the lamb.
    - If desired, add the chicken or lamb stock to the dish for extra moisture.
5. **Cover and Bake:**
    - Cover the baking dish tightly with foil or a lid.
    - Place in the preheated oven and cook for about 3-4 hours, or until the lamb is very tender and easily pulls apart with a fork.
6. **Serve:**
    - Once cooked, remove from the oven and let it rest for a few minutes.
    - Serve the Kleftiko hot, with the roasted potatoes and onions on the side.

Serving Suggestions:

- Kleftiko is traditionally served with a Greek salad and crusty bread.
- You can also serve it with tzatziki sauce and lemon wedges for extra flavor.

Enjoy this flavorful and tender Greek dish that's perfect for sharing with friends and family!

Saganaki (Fried Cheese)

Ingredients:

- 200g (7 oz) Greek cheese suitable for frying (e.g., Kefalotyri, Kasseri, or Halloumi)
- 2-3 tbsp all-purpose flour
- 2-3 tbsp olive oil
- 1-2 tbsp lemon juice (optional)
- Freshly ground black pepper
- Chopped fresh herbs (e.g., parsley, oregano) for garnish (optional)

Instructions:

1. **Prepare the Cheese:**
    - If using a block of cheese, slice it into pieces about 1 cm (0.4 inch) thick. If using a cheese that comes pre-sliced, such as Halloumi, you can use it as is.
2. **Coat with Flour:**
    - Place the flour on a plate or shallow dish.
    - Coat each piece of cheese in flour, shaking off any excess.
3. **Fry the Cheese:**
    - Heat the olive oil in a non-stick skillet or frying pan over medium-high heat.
    - Once the oil is hot, carefully add the cheese pieces in a single layer.
    - Fry for about 2-3 minutes on each side, or until the cheese is golden brown and crispy.
4. **Serve:**
    - Transfer the fried cheese to a serving plate.
    - Squeeze some lemon juice over the cheese if desired.
    - Sprinkle with freshly ground black pepper and chopped fresh herbs for garnish.
5. **Enjoy:**
    - Serve the Saganaki immediately while it's hot and gooey inside. It's best enjoyed as a starter with crusty bread or pita bread.

Serving Suggestions:

- Saganaki is often served with a wedge of lemon to squeeze over the cheese, which adds a tangy freshness to complement the richness of the fried cheese.
- You can also serve it with some olives, cherry tomatoes, or a simple Greek salad on the side for a complete appetizer experience.

This dish is quick to prepare and always delights with its crispy exterior and creamy interior. Perfect for sharing at any gathering or as a treat for yourself!

Melitzanosalata (Eggplant Dip)

Ingredients:

- 2 medium eggplants
- 2-3 cloves garlic, minced
- 1/4 cup extra virgin olive oil, plus extra for drizzling
- 2 tbsp lemon juice (adjust to taste)
- 1/4 cup fresh parsley, finely chopped
- Salt and pepper, to taste
- Optional: pinch of crushed red pepper flakes for a bit of heat
- Optional garnishes: chopped fresh parsley, olives, or a sprinkle of paprika

Instructions:

1. **Prepare the Eggplants:**
    - Preheat your oven to 200°C (400°F).
    - Pierce the eggplants a few times with a fork or knife to prevent bursting during roasting.
    - Place the eggplants on a baking sheet lined with parchment paper or foil.
    - Roast the eggplants in the oven for about 45-60 minutes, turning them occasionally, until the skin is charred and the flesh is very soft.
2. **Cool and Peel:**
    - Remove the eggplants from the oven and let them cool until they are safe to handle.
    - Once cooled, peel off the charred skin from the eggplants. The flesh should be soft and almost creamy.
3. **Prepare the Dip:**
    - Place the peeled eggplant flesh in a colander or strainer to drain excess liquid for about 10-15 minutes.
4. **Blend the Ingredients:**
    - In a food processor or blender, combine the drained eggplant flesh, minced garlic, olive oil, lemon juice, chopped parsley, salt, pepper, and optional red pepper flakes.
    - Pulse or blend until the mixture is smooth and creamy. Taste and adjust seasoning as needed, adding more lemon juice, salt, or pepper according to your preference.
5. **Serve:**
    - Transfer the melitzanosalata to a serving bowl.
    - Drizzle with a little extra olive oil and garnish with chopped parsley, olives, or a sprinkle of paprika if desired.
    - Serve the dip at room temperature or chilled with pita bread, crusty bread, or vegetable sticks.

Tips:

- For a smokier flavor, you can roast the eggplants directly over a gas flame or on a barbecue grill instead of baking them in the oven.
- Adjust the consistency of the dip by adding more olive oil or a splash of water if it seems too thick.
- Melitzanosalata can be stored in an airtight container in the refrigerator for up to 4-5 days. Allow it to come to room temperature before serving leftovers.

Enjoy this creamy and flavorful eggplant dip as part of your Greek-inspired meal or as a tasty appetizer!

Revithosoupa (Chickpea Soup)

Ingredients:

- 1 cup dried chickpeas, soaked overnight (or use canned chickpeas, drained and rinsed)
- 1 onion, finely chopped
- 3 cloves garlic, minced
- 1/4 cup extra virgin olive oil
- 1 bay leaf
- 1 tsp dried oregano
- 1/2 tsp ground cumin
- Salt and pepper, to taste
- Water or vegetable broth, as needed (about 4-5 cups)
- Optional: lemon wedges, chopped fresh parsley for garnish

Instructions:

1. **Prepare the Chickpeas:**
   - If using dried chickpeas, soak them overnight in plenty of water. Drain and rinse the chickpeas before using.
   - If using canned chickpeas, drain and rinse them under cold water.
2. **Cook the Soup:**
   - In a large pot or Dutch oven, heat the olive oil over medium heat.
   - Add the chopped onion and sauté until softened and translucent, about 5-7 minutes.
   - Add the minced garlic and sauté for another minute until fragrant.
3. **Add Chickpeas and Herbs:**
   - Add the drained chickpeas to the pot.
   - Stir in the bay leaf, dried oregano, ground cumin, salt, and pepper.
4. **Cooking the Soup:**
   - Pour enough water or vegetable broth into the pot to cover the chickpeas by about 2 inches.
   - Bring the soup to a boil over medium-high heat.
   - Reduce the heat to low, cover partially with a lid, and simmer gently for about 1.5 to 2 hours, or until the chickpeas are very tender. If using canned chickpeas, simmer for about 30 minutes to allow flavors to meld.
5. **Adjust Seasoning:**
   - Taste and adjust seasoning with more salt and pepper if needed.
6. **Serve:**
   - Ladle the revithosoupa into bowls.
   - Garnish with a drizzle of extra virgin olive oil, a squeeze of fresh lemon juice if desired, and chopped fresh parsley.
   - Serve hot with crusty bread or pita bread.

Tips:

- For a richer flavor, you can sauté the onions until they are caramelized before adding the garlic.
- Feel free to customize the soup by adding carrots, celery, or potatoes for additional texture and flavor.
- Leftover revithosoupa can be stored in the refrigerator for up to 4-5 days. It may thicken upon standing, so add a splash of water when reheating if necessary.

Enjoy this hearty and nutritious Greek chickpea soup as a main dish or a comforting appetizer!

Kalitsounia (Sweet Cheese Pastries)

Dough Ingredients:

- 500g (about 4 cups) all-purpose flour
- 200g (about 7 oz) unsalted butter, softened
- 200g (about 1 cup) Greek yogurt
- 1/4 cup granulated sugar
- Zest of 1 lemon
- 1 tsp baking powder
- Pinch of salt

Filling Ingredients:

- 400g (about 14 oz) ricotta cheese or fresh Greek mizithra cheese
- 100g (about 1/2 cup) granulated sugar
- 1 egg, beaten
- 1/2 tsp vanilla extract
- Zest of 1 lemon
- Optional: 1-2 tbsp raisins soaked in warm water and drained (for added sweetness and texture)

To Finish:

- Powdered sugar, for dusting

Instructions:

1. **Prepare the Dough:**
    - In a large mixing bowl, combine the softened butter and sugar. Mix until creamy and well combined.
    - Add the Greek yogurt and mix until incorporated.
    - Gradually add the flour, baking powder, lemon zest, and a pinch of salt. Mix until a dough forms. If the dough is too sticky, add a little more flour.
    - Knead the dough for a few minutes until smooth. Wrap it in plastic wrap and let it rest in the refrigerator for at least 30 minutes.
2. **Make the Filling:**
    - In another bowl, combine the ricotta or mizithra cheese with the granulated sugar, beaten egg, vanilla extract, lemon zest, and soaked raisins (if using). Mix well until smooth and creamy.
3. **Assemble the Kalitsounia:**
    - Preheat your oven to 180°C (350°F) and line a baking sheet with parchment paper.

- Take a portion of the dough and roll it out on a lightly floured surface to about 1/8 inch thickness.
- Use a round cookie cutter or a glass (about 3-4 inches in diameter) to cut out circles of dough.
- Place a spoonful of the cheese filling in the center of each dough circle.
- Fold the edges of the dough up and around the filling, pinching them together to seal into a crescent shape. You can also fold and twist the edges for a decorative look.

4. **Bake the Kalitsounia:**
   - Place the filled pastries on the prepared baking sheet.
   - Bake in the preheated oven for about 20-25 minutes, or until the kalitsounia are golden brown.

5. **Finish and Serve:**
   - Remove the kalitsounia from the oven and let them cool slightly on a wire rack.
   - Dust with powdered sugar before serving.

Tips:

- You can adjust the sweetness of the filling by adding more or less sugar, according to your taste.
- Kalitsounia can be stored in an airtight container at room temperature for a few days. They are best enjoyed fresh or slightly warmed.

These sweet cheese kalitsounia make a wonderful treat for any occasion, combining the richness of cheese with a delicate pastry crust. Enjoy them with a cup of Greek coffee or tea for a delightful Mediterranean experience!

Gemista (Stuffed Vegetables)

Ingredients:

- 6 large tomatoes
- 4-6 bell peppers (red, yellow, or green)
- 2-3 small zucchini
- 1 onion, finely chopped
- 2 cloves garlic, minced
- 1 cup long-grain rice (such as Greek or Arborio rice)
- 200g (about 7 oz) ground beef or lamb (optional)
- 1/4 cup olive oil, plus extra for drizzling
- 1/4 cup fresh parsley, chopped
- 1/4 cup fresh mint, chopped
- 2 tbsp tomato paste
- 1/2 cup water or vegetable broth
- Salt and pepper, to taste
- Optional: 1/2 cup pine nuts or raisins for extra texture and sweetness

Instructions:

1. **Prepare the Vegetables:**
   - Preheat your oven to 180°C (350°F).
   - Cut the tops off the tomatoes and set them aside. Scoop out the flesh and seeds from the tomatoes using a spoon, being careful not to puncture the skin. Reserve the flesh and juices.
   - Cut the tops off the bell peppers and remove the seeds and membranes.
   - Cut the zucchini in half lengthwise and scoop out the flesh, leaving a shell to stuff.

2. **Prepare the Filling:**
   - In a large bowl, combine the rice, chopped onion, minced garlic, chopped parsley, chopped mint, and optional ground meat (if using).
   - Heat 2 tablespoons of olive oil in a large skillet over medium heat. Add the rice mixture and sauté for 3-4 minutes until the onions are translucent and the rice is lightly toasted.
   - Add the tomato paste and cook for another minute, stirring to combine.
   - Pour in the reserved tomato flesh and juices (strained if necessary) and the water or vegetable broth.
   - Season with salt and pepper to taste. Stir well and simmer for about 5-7 minutes until the liquid is absorbed and the rice is partially cooked. Remove from heat.

3. **Stuff and Bake the Vegetables:**
   - Lightly drizzle the inside of each vegetable shell with olive oil and season with salt and pepper.

- Fill each tomato, bell pepper, and zucchini shell with the rice mixture, pressing down gently to pack it in.
- Place the stuffed vegetables in a baking dish. If you have leftover filling, you can place it around the vegetables in the dish.
- Drizzle the tops of the stuffed vegetables with a little more olive oil.

4. **Bake:**
    - Cover the baking dish with aluminum foil and bake in the preheated oven for about 45-60 minutes, or until the vegetables are tender and the rice is fully cooked.
    - If you prefer a bit of char on the vegetables, you can remove the foil during the last 15 minutes of baking.

5. **Serve:**
    - Remove from the oven and let the gemista cool slightly before serving.
    - Serve warm or at room temperature. They can be enjoyed on their own or with a side of Greek yogurt or a fresh salad.

Tips:

- You can customize the filling by adding pine nuts, raisins, or other dried fruits for added texture and sweetness.
- Gemista can be made vegetarian by omitting the meat and using vegetable broth instead of water.
- Leftover gemista can be stored in an airtight container in the refrigerator for up to 3-4 days. They can be reheated gently in the oven or microwave before serving.

Gemista is a hearty and satisfying dish that showcases the flavors of fresh vegetables and Mediterranean herbs. It's perfect for sharing with family and friends!

Keftedes (Greek Meatballs)

Ingredients:

For the Meatballs:

- 500g (about 1 lb) ground beef or a mixture of beef and pork
- 1 small onion, finely chopped or grated
- 2 cloves garlic, minced
- 1/2 cup breadcrumbs
- 1/4 cup fresh parsley, finely chopped
- 1/4 cup fresh mint, finely chopped (optional)
- 1/4 cup grated Parmesan cheese (optional)
- 1 egg, beaten
- 1 tsp dried oregano
- 1/2 tsp ground cumin
- Salt and pepper, to taste
- Olive oil, for frying

For Serving:

- Tzatziki sauce or Greek yogurt sauce (optional)
- Lemon wedges
- Fresh parsley, chopped for garnish (optional)

Instructions:

1. **Prepare the Meatball Mixture:**
   - In a large mixing bowl, combine the ground meat, chopped onion, minced garlic, breadcrumbs, parsley, mint (if using), Parmesan cheese (if using), beaten egg, dried oregano, ground cumin, salt, and pepper.
   - Mix everything together well using your hands, ensuring that all ingredients are evenly distributed.
2. **Shape the Meatballs:**
   - Take small portions of the mixture and roll them into meatballs, about 1-2 inches in diameter. You can wet your hands slightly with water to prevent sticking.
3. **Fry the Meatballs:**
   - Heat a generous amount of olive oil in a large skillet or frying pan over medium heat.
   - Once the oil is hot, add the meatballs in batches, making sure not to overcrowd the pan. Cook them in batches if necessary.
   - Fry the meatballs for about 4-5 minutes on each side, or until they are golden brown and cooked through. You may need to adjust the heat to ensure they cook evenly without burning.
4. **Serve:**

- Once cooked, remove the meatballs from the pan and place them on a plate lined with paper towels to absorb any excess oil.
- Serve the keftedes hot with tzatziki sauce or Greek yogurt sauce on the side for dipping.
- Garnish with lemon wedges and chopped fresh parsley if desired.

Tips:

- If you prefer baking instead of frying, you can place the meatballs on a baking sheet lined with parchment paper and bake them in a preheated oven at 200°C (400°F) for about 15-20 minutes, or until they are cooked through and golden brown.
- For extra flavor, you can add a pinch of ground cinnamon or nutmeg to the meatball mixture.
- Leftover keftedes can be stored in an airtight container in the refrigerator for up to 3-4 days. They can be reheated gently in the oven or microwave before serving.

Enjoy these flavorful Greek meatballs as an appetizer, part of a meze spread, or as a main dish with a side of Greek salad and crusty bread!

Galaktoboureko (Custard Pie)

Ingredients:

For the Custard Filling:

- 1 liter (4 cups) whole milk
- 150g (3/4 cup) fine semolina flour
- 150g (3/4 cup) granulated sugar
- 4 large eggs
- 1 tsp vanilla extract
- Zest of 1 lemon
- 50g (1/4 cup) unsalted butter

For the Pastry:

- 1 package of phyllo pastry sheets (about 400g or 14 oz), thawed if frozen
- 200g (about 7 oz) unsalted butter, melted

For the Syrup:

- 300g (1 1/2 cups) granulated sugar
- 250ml (1 cup) water
- Juice of 1/2 lemon
- Optional: 1 cinnamon stick, 1-2 cloves, or a splash of vanilla extract for flavor

Instructions:

1. **Prepare the Custard Filling:**
    - In a large saucepan, heat the milk over medium heat until it comes to a simmer. Remove from heat.
    - In a separate bowl, whisk together the semolina flour and sugar.
    - Add the eggs to the semolina mixture and whisk until smooth and well combined.
    - Slowly pour the hot milk into the semolina mixture, whisking constantly to prevent lumps.
    - Return the mixture to the saucepan and place it over medium-low heat.
    - Cook, stirring constantly with a wooden spoon, until the mixture thickens and resembles a smooth custard, about 10-15 minutes.
    - Remove from heat and stir in the vanilla extract, lemon zest, and butter until the butter is melted and fully incorporated. Set aside to cool slightly.
2. **Assemble the Galaktoboureko:**
    - Preheat your oven to 180°C (350°F). Lightly grease a large baking dish (about 9x13 inches) with butter.
    - Lay half of the phyllo sheets in the baking dish, brushing each sheet generously with melted butter. Fold any excess overhanging phyllo back into the dish.

- Pour the custard filling over the phyllo pastry and spread it out evenly with a spatula.
3. **Layer the Remaining Phyllo:**
   - Place the remaining phyllo sheets on top of the custard filling, again brushing each sheet generously with melted butter.
   - Trim any excess phyllo that hangs over the edges of the dish.
4. **Bake:**
   - Using a sharp knife, score the top layer of phyllo into diamond or square shapes, being careful not to cut all the way through to the custard.
   - Bake in the preheated oven for about 45-50 minutes, or until the phyllo is crisp and golden brown.
5. **Make the Syrup:**
   - While the Galaktoboureko is baking, prepare the syrup. In a small saucepan, combine the sugar, water, lemon juice, and any optional spices (cinnamon stick, cloves, or vanilla extract).
   - Bring the mixture to a boil over medium-high heat, stirring occasionally until the sugar is completely dissolved.
   - Reduce the heat to low and simmer for about 5-7 minutes, or until the syrup slightly thickens.
6. **Finish:**
   - Once the Galaktoboureko is baked and golden brown, remove it from the oven.
   - Immediately pour the warm syrup over the hot pastry, allowing it to soak in thoroughly.
   - Let the Galaktoboureko cool completely in the baking dish before slicing and serving.

Serving:

- Serve Galaktoboureko at room temperature or slightly chilled.
- Cut into squares or diamond shapes along the scored lines.
- Optionally, sprinkle with powdered sugar or ground cinnamon before serving.

Tips:

- Phyllo pastry can dry out quickly, so keep it covered with a damp towel while you're working with it.
- Be careful when pouring the hot syrup over the hot pastry to ensure even soaking.
- Leftover Galaktoboureko can be stored covered in the refrigerator for up to 3-4 days. Enjoy it as a sweet treat with coffee or tea!

This recipe captures the essence of traditional Greek cuisine with its layers of crispy pastry and creamy custard, finished with a sweet syrup that makes every bite irresistible. Enjoy making and sharing this classic dessert with family and friends!

Patsas (Tripe Soup)

Ingredients:

- 1 kg (about 2.2 lbs) beef tripe, thoroughly cleaned and cut into small pieces
- 1 onion, finely chopped
- 2-3 cloves garlic, minced
- 2 tbsp olive oil
- 1/2 cup white wine (optional)
- 2-3 liters (8-12 cups) water or beef broth
- 1/2 cup rice, rinsed (optional)
- Salt and pepper, to taste
- 1-2 tbsp vinegar (optional, for cleaning the tripe)
- Lemon wedges, chopped fresh parsley, and dried oregano for serving

Instructions:

1. **Prepare the Tripe:**
   - If the tripe is not already cleaned by the butcher, rinse it thoroughly under cold water and scrub gently with a brush to remove any residue.
   - Optionally, soak the tripe in water with a tablespoon or two of vinegar for about an hour. This can help reduce any strong odor.
2. **Cook the Tripe:**
   - In a large pot, heat the olive oil over medium heat.
   - Add the chopped onion and minced garlic. Sauté until the onion is soft and translucent.
3. **Add the Tripe:**
   - Add the cleaned tripe pieces to the pot. Sauté for a few minutes until lightly browned.
4. **Deglaze and Simmer:**
   - If using white wine, pour it into the pot and stir, scraping up any browned bits from the bottom.
   - Add water or beef broth to cover the tripe by a few inches. Bring to a boil.
5. **Simmer:**
   - Reduce the heat to low and let the soup simmer gently, partially covered, for about 2-3 hours or until the tripe is tender and cooked through. Skim off any foam that rises to the surface.
6. **Optional: Add Rice**
   - If using rice, add it to the pot about 20-30 minutes before the soup is done. Cook until the rice is tender.
7. **Season and Serve:**
   - Season the soup with salt and pepper to taste.
   - Serve hot, garnished with lemon wedges, chopped fresh parsley, and a sprinkle of dried oregano.

- Patsas is traditionally served with crusty bread and sometimes a side of vinegar or hot pepper flakes for extra flavor.

Tips:

- Patsas is often enjoyed as a comforting dish after late-night outings, as it is believed to aid in digestion and provide nourishment.
- Adjust the cooking time based on the tenderness of the tripe; it should be soft and tender but not overcooked.
- Leftover Patsas can be stored in the refrigerator for up to 3-4 days. Reheat gently on the stovetop, adding a splash of water or broth if needed.

Enjoy this traditional Greek tripe soup as a hearty and warming dish, perfect for colder days or as a unique culinary experience!

Koulourakia (Butter Cookies)

Ingredients:

- 250g (about 2 cups) all-purpose flour
- 1/2 tsp baking powder
- 1/4 tsp salt
- 150g (2/3 cup) unsalted butter, softened
- 150g (3/4 cup) granulated sugar
- 2 large eggs
- 1 tsp vanilla extract
- Zest of 1 lemon (optional, for extra flavor)
- 1 egg yolk, beaten (for brushing)

Instructions:

1. **Preheat Oven and Prepare Baking Sheets:**
   - Preheat your oven to 180°C (350°F). Line baking sheets with parchment paper.
2. **Prepare Dry Ingredients:**
   - In a medium bowl, whisk together the flour, baking powder, and salt. Set aside.
3. **Cream Butter and Sugar:**
   - In a large bowl or using a stand mixer fitted with the paddle attachment, cream together the softened butter and sugar until light and fluffy.
4. **Add Eggs and Flavorings:**
   - Add the eggs one at a time, mixing well after each addition.
   - Mix in the vanilla extract and lemon zest (if using).
5. **Combine Wet and Dry Ingredients:**
   - Gradually add the flour mixture to the butter mixture, mixing until a soft dough forms. The dough should be smooth and slightly sticky.
6. **Shape the Cookies:**
   - Take a small portion of dough (about 1 tablespoon) and roll it into a rope about 5 inches long.
   - Shape the rope into a twist, braid, or circle, pressing the ends lightly to seal. You can also shape them into coils or S-shapes.
   - Place the shaped cookies on the prepared baking sheets, leaving some space between them.
7. **Brush with Egg Yolk:**
   - Brush the tops of the cookies with beaten egg yolk. This will give them a golden sheen when baked.
8. **Bake:**
   - Bake the cookies in the preheated oven for about 12-15 minutes, or until they are golden brown on the bottom and edges.
   - Remove from the oven and let them cool on the baking sheets for a few minutes before transferring to a wire rack to cool completely.

9. **Serve and Store:**
    - Once cooled, store the Koulourakia in an airtight container at room temperature.
    - They can be enjoyed plain or dipped in coffee, tea, or milk.

Tips:

- You can customize the flavor of Koulourakia by adding different extracts such as almond or orange, or incorporating spices like cinnamon or nutmeg.
- These cookies keep well for several days in an airtight container, making them perfect for sharing or gifting during holidays.

Enjoy these delightful Greek butter cookies with their distinctive shapes and flavors, perfect for any festive occasion or as a sweet treat with your afternoon tea!

Arni Lemonato (Lamb with Lemon Sauce)

Ingredients:

- 1.5 kg (about 3.3 lbs) lamb shoulder or leg, cut into chunks
- 3-4 tbsp olive oil
- 1 large onion, finely chopped
- 4 cloves garlic, minced
- 1/2 cup dry white wine
- 1/2 cup chicken broth or water
- Zest of 1-2 lemons
- Juice of 2 lemons
- 2 tbsp fresh oregano, chopped (or 1 tbsp dried oregano)
- Salt and pepper, to taste
- Fresh parsley, chopped for garnish

Instructions:

1. **Preheat Oven:**
   - Preheat your oven to 180°C (350°F).
2. **Sear the Lamb:**
   - Season the lamb pieces generously with salt and pepper.
   - In a large oven-safe pot or Dutch oven, heat the olive oil over medium-high heat.
   - Add the lamb pieces in batches and sear them on all sides until browned. Remove and set aside.
3. **Cook the Aromatics:**
   - In the same pot, add the chopped onion and sauté until softened and translucent, about 5 minutes.
   - Add the minced garlic and cook for another minute until fragrant.
4. **Deglaze and Simmer:**
   - Pour in the white wine and scrape up any browned bits from the bottom of the pot.
   - Add the chicken broth or water, lemon zest, lemon juice, and oregano. Stir to combine.
5. **Braise the Lamb:**
   - Return the lamb pieces to the pot, along with any juices that have accumulated.
   - Cover the pot with a lid and place it in the preheated oven.
6. **Bake:**
   - Braise the lamb in the oven for about 2.5 to 3 hours, or until the meat is fork-tender and begins to fall off the bone. Check and stir occasionally, adding more liquid if necessary to keep it from drying out.
7. **Finish and Serve:**
   - Once the lamb is cooked through and tender, remove it from the oven.
   - Taste and adjust seasoning with salt and pepper if needed.

- Serve the lamb hot, garnished with chopped fresh parsley.

Serving Suggestions:

- Arni Lemonato pairs wonderfully with traditional Greek sides such as roasted potatoes, rice pilaf, or a Greek salad.
- You can also serve it with crusty bread to soak up the delicious lemony sauce.

Tips:

- For a thicker sauce, you can remove the lamb pieces from the pot once cooked and simmer the sauce on the stovetop until it reduces to your desired consistency.
- This dish can also be made with other cuts of lamb or even chicken if preferred.

Enjoy this flavorful and comforting Greek dish of Arni Lemonato, perfect for sharing with family and friends on special occasions or gatherings!

Horta Vrasta (Boiled Greens)

Ingredients:

- 1 kg (about 2.2 lbs) mixed greens (such as dandelion greens, spinach, chicory, Swiss chard, or a combination)
- Water, enough to cover the greens in a large pot
- Salt, to taste
- Extra virgin olive oil, for drizzling (optional)
- Lemon wedges, for serving

Instructions:

1. **Prepare the Greens:**
   - Rinse the greens thoroughly under cold water to remove any dirt or grit.
   - Trim off any tough stems or thick parts, if necessary.
   - If using dandelion greens, blanch them in boiling water for about 5 minutes to reduce bitterness. Drain and rinse with cold water.
2. **Boil the Greens:**
   - In a large pot, bring enough water to cover the greens to a boil.
   - Add a generous pinch of salt to the boiling water.
   - Add the greens to the boiling water. If using a mix of greens, add the tougher greens first (like dandelion greens or Swiss chard) and then add the more tender greens (like spinach) a few minutes later.
   - Boil the greens for about 10-15 minutes, or until they are tender but still vibrant green. Stir occasionally to ensure even cooking.
3. **Drain and Serve:**
   - Once the greens are cooked to your liking, drain them well using a colander or slotted spoon.
   - Transfer the cooked greens to a serving plate or bowl.
4. **Serve:**
   - Drizzle the Horta Vrasta with extra virgin olive oil, if desired.
   - Serve hot or at room temperature with lemon wedges on the side for squeezing over the greens.

Serving Suggestions:

- Horta Vrasta can be served as a side dish alongside grilled meats, fish, or other Greek dishes.
- It's also delicious with crusty bread and feta cheese, or as part of a meze platter.

Tips:

- To add more flavor, you can sauté some minced garlic in olive oil and toss the cooked greens in the garlic-infused oil before serving.
- Leftover Horta Vrasta can be stored in an airtight container in the refrigerator for a few days. Reheat gently before serving.

Enjoy this simple and nutritious Greek dish of Horta Vrasta, showcasing the fresh flavors of greens with a touch of olive oil and lemon!

Yemista (Stuffed Peppers)

Ingredients:

- 6 large bell peppers (red, yellow, or green)
- 1 cup long-grain rice (such as Greek or Arborio rice)
- 200g (about 7 oz) ground beef or lamb (optional)
- 1 onion, finely chopped
- 2 cloves garlic, minced
- 1/4 cup olive oil, plus extra for drizzling
- 1/4 cup fresh parsley, chopped
- 1/4 cup fresh mint, chopped
- 2 tbsp tomato paste
- 1/2 cup water or vegetable broth
- Salt and pepper, to taste
- Optional: 1/2 cup pine nuts or raisins for extra texture and sweetness

Instructions:

1. **Prepare the Bell Peppers:**
    - Preheat your oven to 180°C (350°F).
    - Cut the tops off the bell peppers and remove the seeds and membranes.
    - Rinse the bell peppers under cold water and pat dry with a paper towel.
2. **Prepare the Filling:**
    - In a large bowl, combine the rice, chopped onion, minced garlic, chopped parsley, chopped mint, and optional ground meat (if using).
    - Heat 2 tablespoons of olive oil in a large skillet over medium heat. Add the rice mixture and sauté for 3-4 minutes until the onions are translucent and the rice is lightly toasted.
    - Add the tomato paste and cook for another minute, stirring to combine.
    - Pour in the water or vegetable broth. Season with salt and pepper to taste. Stir well and simmer for about 5-7 minutes until the liquid is absorbed and the rice is partially cooked. Remove from heat.
3. **Fill the Bell Peppers:**
    - Lightly drizzle the inside of each bell pepper with olive oil and season with salt and pepper.
    - Fill each bell pepper with the rice mixture, pressing down gently to pack it in. If there is any leftover filling, you can place it around the bell peppers in the baking dish.
4. **Bake:**
    - Place the stuffed bell peppers upright in a baking dish. Drizzle the tops with a little more olive oil.

- Cover the baking dish with aluminum foil and bake in the preheated oven for about 45-60 minutes, or until the bell peppers are tender and the rice is fully cooked.
- If you prefer a bit of char on the bell peppers, you can remove the foil during the last 15 minutes of baking.

5. **Serve:**
   - Remove from the oven and let the stuffed bell peppers cool slightly before serving.
   - Serve warm as a main dish or as part of a Greek meze spread.

Tips:

- You can customize the filling by adding pine nuts, raisins, or other dried fruits for added texture and sweetness.
- Yemista can be made vegetarian by omitting the meat and using vegetable broth instead of water.
- Leftover stuffed bell peppers can be stored in an airtight container in the refrigerator for up to 3-4 days. They can be reheated gently in the oven or microwave before serving.

Yemista is a comforting and flavorful dish that showcases the vibrant flavors of Greek cuisine. Enjoy these stuffed bell peppers with their hearty rice filling and aromatic herbs!

Psarosoupa (Fish Soup)

Ingredients:

- 500g (about 1 lb) mixed seafood (such as white fish fillets, shrimp, calamari, mussels, or any combination)
- 1 onion, finely chopped
- 2-3 cloves garlic, minced
- 2 carrots, diced
- 2 celery stalks, diced
- 1 potato, peeled and diced
- 1 red bell pepper, diced
- 2 tomatoes, diced
- 1/4 cup olive oil
- 1/2 cup dry white wine
- 1.5 liters (6 cups) fish or vegetable broth
- 1 bay leaf
- 1 tsp dried oregano
- Salt and pepper, to taste
- Fresh parsley, chopped, for garnish
- Lemon wedges, for serving

Instructions:

1. **Prepare the Seafood:**
   - Clean and prepare the seafood as needed. Cut fish fillets into bite-sized pieces. Clean and devein shrimp if necessary. Prepare calamari tubes by slicing into rings.
2. **Sauté the Aromatics:**
   - In a large pot or Dutch oven, heat the olive oil over medium heat.
   - Add the chopped onion, minced garlic, diced carrots, celery, and red bell pepper. Sauté for 5-7 minutes until the vegetables are softened.
3. **Add Tomatoes and Potatoes:**
   - Stir in the diced tomatoes and potatoes. Cook for another 2-3 minutes.
4. **Deglaze with Wine:**
   - Pour in the white wine and let it simmer for a minute or two to evaporate the alcohol.
5. **Add Broth and Seasonings:**
   - Add the fish or vegetable broth to the pot.
   - Stir in the bay leaf, dried oregano, salt, and pepper to taste.
6. **Simmer the Soup:**
   - Bring the soup to a boil, then reduce the heat to low and let it simmer uncovered for about 15-20 minutes, or until the potatoes are tender.
7. **Add Seafood:**

- Add the seafood to the pot. Cook for 5-7 minutes, or until the seafood is cooked through. Be careful not to overcook the seafood as it can become tough.
8. **Serve:**
    - Remove the bay leaf from the soup.
    - Ladle the Psarosoupa into bowls. Garnish with chopped fresh parsley.
    - Serve hot with lemon wedges on the side for squeezing over the soup.

Tips:

- Choose a variety of seafood that you enjoy and that is fresh and in season. Feel free to customize the mix based on availability.
- You can adjust the thickness of the soup by adding more or less broth according to your preference.
- Psarosoupa is traditionally served with crusty bread to soak up the delicious broth.

Enjoy this comforting and flavorful Greek fish soup, Psarosoupa, which brings together the freshness of seafood with aromatic vegetables and herbs!

Melomakarona (Honey Cookies)

Ingredients:

For the Cookies:

- 1 cup vegetable oil
- 1/2 cup sugar
- 1/2 cup fresh orange juice
- Zest of 1 orange
- 1/4 cup brandy or cognac (optional)
- 1 tsp ground cinnamon
- 1/2 tsp ground cloves
- 1/2 tsp baking soda
- 1 tsp baking powder
- 4 cups all-purpose flour (plus extra if needed)

For the Syrup:

- 1 cup honey
- 1 cup water
- 1 cup sugar
- Optional: Whole cloves, cinnamon stick, or orange peel for flavoring the syrup

For Garnish:

- Chopped walnuts or almonds, for sprinkling

Instructions:

1. **Make the Dough:**
    - In a large mixing bowl, whisk together the vegetable oil and sugar until well combined.
    - Add the fresh orange juice, orange zest, brandy (if using), ground cinnamon, and ground cloves. Mix well.
    - In a separate small bowl, dissolve the baking soda in 1 tablespoon of warm water. Add it to the oil and sugar mixture and mix again.
    - Gradually add the flour and baking powder to the mixture, mixing with a spoon or your hands until a soft dough forms. The dough should be soft and slightly sticky but manageable. Add more flour if needed, but be careful not to overmix.
2. **Shape the Cookies:**
    - Take a small portion of dough (about the size of a walnut) and roll it into an oval or egg shape. Place it on a baking sheet lined with parchment paper.
    - Use a fork to press lightly on the top of each cookie to create a pattern.
3. **Bake:**

- Preheat your oven to 180°C (350°F).
- Bake the cookies in the preheated oven for about 20-25 minutes, or until they are golden brown and cooked through. Be careful not to overbake.
4. **Make the Syrup:**
    - While the cookies are baking, prepare the honey syrup. In a medium saucepan, combine the honey, water, and sugar. Add any optional flavorings like cloves, cinnamon stick, or orange peel.
    - Bring the mixture to a boil over medium-high heat, stirring occasionally. Reduce the heat and let it simmer gently for about 5-7 minutes until slightly thickened.
    - Remove from heat and set aside to cool slightly.
5. **Soak the Cookies:**
    - Once the cookies are baked and still warm, immediately dip each cookie into the warm honey syrup for a few seconds, turning to coat evenly.
    - Place the soaked cookies on a wire rack set over a baking sheet (to catch any drips).
6. **Garnish:**
    - Sprinkle the tops of the cookies with chopped walnuts or almonds while the syrup is still sticky.
7. **Serve and Store:**
    - Let the cookies cool completely before serving. Store them in an airtight container at room temperature.
    - Melomakarona are best enjoyed after a day or two, as the flavors meld together and the cookies become even more moist and flavorful.

Tips:

- The syrup should be warm when soaking the cookies, as this helps them absorb the honey syrup effectively.
- You can adjust the amount of honey syrup depending on how soaked you prefer your cookies. Some like them lightly soaked, while others prefer them more moist.
- Melomakarona can be stored in an airtight container at room temperature for up to two weeks.

Enjoy these delicious and aromatic Melomakarona as a delightful treat during the holiday season or any time you crave a taste of Greek sweetness!

Kokoretsi (Offal Dish)

Ingredients:

- 1 set of lamb or goat intestines (cleaned and prepared, can be obtained from a butcher)
- 1 kg (about 2.2 lbs) organ meats (such as heart, lungs, liver, sweetbreads), cleaned and diced
- 1 onion, finely chopped
- 2-3 cloves garlic, minced
- 1/4 cup fresh parsley, finely chopped
- 1/4 cup fresh mint, finely chopped
- 1/4 cup olive oil
- Salt and pepper, to taste
- Lemon wedges, for serving

Instructions:

1. **Prepare the Intestines:**
   - Clean and prepare the lamb or goat intestines by rinsing thoroughly under cold water and soaking them in water with a splash of vinegar for a few hours to remove any residual odor.
2. **Prepare the Filling:**
   - In a large mixing bowl, combine the diced organ meats (heart, lungs, liver, sweetbreads) with the chopped onion, minced garlic, parsley, mint, olive oil, salt, and pepper. Mix well to combine.
3. **Assemble the Kokoretsi:**
   - Lay out the cleaned intestines on a clean work surface. They are usually twisted or braided to form a long tube.
   - Thread the mixed organ meats onto the intestines, wrapping and securing them tightly with kitchen twine or skewers to form a cylindrical shape.
4. **Roast the Kokoretsi:**
   - Traditionally, Kokoretsi is cooked over a charcoal or wood-fired grill. The wrapped meats are placed on a rotisserie spit and roasted slowly over moderate heat.
   - As the Kokoretsi cooks, it's periodically basted with a mixture of olive oil, lemon juice, and herbs to keep it moist and flavorful.
   - Cook the Kokoretsi until the internal temperature reaches at least 70°C (160°F) to ensure that the organ meats are fully cooked.
5. **Serve:**
   - Once cooked, remove the Kokoretsi from the grill and let it rest for a few minutes.
   - Remove the twine or skewers and slice the Kokoretsi into rounds or slices.
   - Serve hot, garnished with lemon wedges and accompanied by crusty bread, Greek salad, and tzatziki sauce.

Tips:

- Kokoretsi is a dish that requires some skill to prepare due to the wrapping and roasting process. It's often made by experienced cooks or purchased from specialty butchers or restaurants.
- The choice of organ meats can vary based on personal preference and availability. Some variations may include kidneys or other offal.

Enjoy Kokoretsi as a unique and flavorful dish that reflects the rich culinary traditions of Greece, especially during festive gatherings and celebrations!

Briam (Greek Ratatouille)

Ingredients:

- 2 large potatoes, peeled and sliced into rounds
- 2 large zucchini, sliced into rounds
- 2 large tomatoes, sliced into rounds
- 1 large red onion, thinly sliced
- 1 red bell pepper, sliced into strips
- 1 green bell pepper, sliced into strips
- 2-3 garlic cloves, minced
- 1/4 cup extra virgin olive oil
- 1 tsp dried oregano
- 1 tsp dried thyme
- Salt and pepper, to taste
- Fresh parsley, chopped, for garnish

Instructions:

1. **Preheat Oven:**
    - Preheat your oven to 180°C (350°F).
2. **Prepare the Vegetables:**
    - In a large baking dish or roasting pan, arrange the sliced potatoes, zucchini, tomatoes, red onion, and bell peppers in layers or mixed together.
3. **Season:**
    - Sprinkle minced garlic over the vegetables.
    - Drizzle olive oil evenly over the vegetables.
    - Season with dried oregano, dried thyme, salt, and pepper to taste. Toss gently to coat the vegetables with the oil and seasonings.
4. **Bake:**
    - Cover the baking dish with aluminum foil and place it in the preheated oven.
    - Bake for about 45-60 minutes, or until the vegetables are tender and lightly caramelized, stirring once halfway through cooking.
5. **Serve:**
    - Remove from the oven and let it cool slightly.
    - Garnish with chopped fresh parsley before serving.

Tips:

- Briam can be served warm or at room temperature.
- You can adjust the vegetables based on what you have on hand or personal preference. Eggplants are also commonly used in Briam.
- Leftover Briam can be stored in an airtight container in the refrigerator for a few days. It can be reheated gently in the oven or microwave.

Briam is a versatile dish that can be served as a main course with crusty bread, as a side dish to grilled meats, or even as part of a mezze spread. Enjoy this flavorful Greek vegetable bake that celebrates the bounty of fresh produce!

Bougatsa (Cream Pie)

Ingredients:

For the Custard Filling:

- 4 cups whole milk
- 1 cup granulated sugar
- 1/2 cup semolina flour
- 1/4 tsp salt
- 1 tsp vanilla extract
- Zest of 1 lemon
- 4 large eggs

For the Bougatsa:

- 1 package (about 400g) phyllo dough, thawed if frozen
- 1 cup unsalted butter, melted
- Powdered sugar, for dusting
- Ground cinnamon, for dusting

Instructions:

1. **Make the Custard Filling:**
    - In a saucepan, heat the milk over medium heat until it starts to simmer. Add the sugar and stir until dissolved.
    - Gradually whisk in the semolina flour, salt, vanilla extract, and lemon zest. Cook over medium heat, stirring constantly, until the mixture thickens (about 5-7 minutes). Remove from heat and let it cool slightly.
    - In a separate bowl, whisk the eggs. Gradually add a small amount of the warm semolina mixture to the eggs, whisking constantly to temper the eggs.
    - Pour the tempered egg mixture back into the saucepan with the remaining semolina mixture. Cook over medium-low heat, stirring constantly, until the custard thickens and coats the back of a spoon (about 2-3 minutes). Remove from heat and let it cool completely.
2. **Prepare the Phyllo Dough:**
    - Preheat your oven to 180°C (350°F).
    - Brush a baking dish (about 9x13 inches) with melted butter.
    - Lay one sheet of phyllo dough in the baking dish and brush it with melted butter. Repeat this process, layering and buttering each sheet of phyllo dough, until you have used about half of the package.
3. **Add the Custard Filling:**
    - Spread the cooled custard evenly over the layered phyllo dough in the baking dish.
4. **Complete the Bougatsa:**

- - Continue layering the remaining sheets of phyllo dough on top of the custard, brushing each sheet with melted butter. Fold any excess phyllo dough from the sides over the top layers.
  - Brush the top layer generously with melted butter.
  - Using a sharp knife, score the top layer of phyllo dough into squares or diamond shapes (this will make it easier to cut after baking).
  - Bake in the preheated oven for about 45-50 minutes, or until the top is golden brown and crisp.
5. **Serve:**
   - Remove from the oven and let it cool slightly.
   - Dust the top with powdered sugar and ground cinnamon.
   - Serve warm or at room temperature, cut into squares or slices.

Tips:

- Phyllo dough can dry out quickly, so cover it with a damp kitchen towel while working with it to prevent it from becoming brittle.
- Bougatsa is best enjoyed fresh, but leftovers can be stored in an airtight container in the refrigerator for a day or two. Reheat gently in the oven before serving.
- Feel free to adjust the sweetness of the custard filling to your preference by adding more or less sugar.

Enjoy making and savoring this delightful Greek pastry, Bougatsa, with its crispy layers and creamy custard filling!

Karidopita (Walnut Cake)

Ingredients:

For the Cake:

- 1 cup walnuts, finely chopped
- 1 cup breadcrumbs (from stale bread)
- 1 cup granulated sugar
- 1 cup all-purpose flour
- 1 tsp baking powder
- 1 tsp ground cinnamon
- 1/2 tsp ground cloves
- 1/4 tsp salt
- Zest of 1 orange
- Zest of 1 lemon
- 4 large eggs
- 1/2 cup vegetable oil
- 1/2 cup milk

For the Syrup:

- 1 cup granulated sugar
- 1 cup water
- 1 cinnamon stick
- Zest of 1 lemon
- Zest of 1 orange
- 1/4 cup honey
- 1/4 cup brandy or cognac (optional)

For Garnish (optional):

- Chopped walnuts
- Whipped cream or vanilla ice cream

Instructions:

1. **Preheat Oven and Prepare Pan:**
   - Preheat your oven to 180°C (350°F). Grease a 9x13 inch baking dish or cake pan and line it with parchment paper.
2. **Make the Cake:**
   - In a large bowl, combine the chopped walnuts, breadcrumbs, sugar, flour, baking powder, ground cinnamon, ground cloves, salt, orange zest, and lemon zest. Mix well.
3. **Prepare the Wet Ingredients:**

- In another bowl, whisk together the eggs, vegetable oil, and milk until well combined.
4. **Combine Dry and Wet Ingredients:**
   - Gradually add the wet ingredients to the dry ingredients, stirring until the batter is smooth and well mixed.
5. **Bake the Cake:**
   - Pour the batter into the prepared baking dish or cake pan, spreading it evenly with a spatula.
   - Bake in the preheated oven for about 35-40 minutes, or until a toothpick inserted into the center of the cake comes out clean.
6. **Make the Syrup:**
   - While the cake is baking, prepare the syrup. In a saucepan, combine the sugar, water, cinnamon stick, lemon zest, and orange zest. Bring to a boil over medium-high heat, stirring occasionally.
   - Reduce the heat and simmer for 5-7 minutes, until the syrup slightly thickens.
   - Remove from heat and stir in the honey and brandy or cognac (if using). Let the syrup cool slightly.
7. **Soak the Cake:**
   - Once the cake is baked and still warm, use a skewer or fork to poke holes all over the top of the cake.
   - Slowly pour the warm syrup over the cake, making sure to evenly distribute it and allow it to soak into the cake. Let the cake absorb the syrup for at least 1 hour.
8. **Garnish and Serve:**
   - Optionally, garnish the top of the cake with chopped walnuts.
   - Serve Karidopita warm or at room temperature, optionally with whipped cream or a scoop of vanilla ice cream.

Tips:

- The longer you allow the cake to soak in the syrup, the more moist and flavorful it will become.
- You can adjust the sweetness of the syrup to your preference by adding more or less sugar.
- Karidopita can be stored in an airtight container at room temperature for a few days. It actually improves in flavor after sitting for a day or two as the flavors meld together.

Enjoy this delicious and aromatic Greek walnut cake, Karidopita, which is perfect for celebrating special occasions or simply enjoying as a sweet treat with a cup of coffee or tea!

Papoutsakia (Stuffed Eggplants)

Ingredients:

For the Eggplants:

- 4 medium-sized eggplants
- Salt
- Olive oil, for brushing

For the Meat Filling:

- 300g (about 10 oz) ground beef or lamb
- 1 onion, finely chopped
- 2 cloves garlic, minced
- 1/2 cup chopped tomatoes (fresh or canned)
- 1 tbsp tomato paste
- 1/2 tsp ground cinnamon
- 1/4 tsp ground nutmeg
- Salt and pepper, to taste
- 1/4 cup chopped fresh parsley
- 1/4 cup breadcrumbs (optional, for binding)

For the Béchamel Sauce:

- 4 tbsp unsalted butter
- 1/4 cup all-purpose flour
- 2 cups milk, warmed
- Salt and pepper, to taste
- Pinch of ground nutmeg
- 1/2 cup grated Parmesan cheese

Instructions:

1. **Prepare the Eggplants:**
    - Preheat your oven to 200°C (400°F).
    - Cut each eggplant in half lengthwise. Score the flesh with a knife in a crisscross pattern, being careful not to cut through the skin.
    - Sprinkle the cut side with salt and let them sit for about 15-20 minutes. This helps draw out excess moisture and bitterness.
    - Rinse the eggplants under cold water and pat them dry with paper towels.
    - Brush the eggplants lightly with olive oil and place them on a baking sheet, cut side down.
    - Bake in the preheated oven for 20-25 minutes, or until they are tender. Remove from the oven and let them cool slightly.

2. **Prepare the Meat Filling:**
   - While the eggplants are baking, prepare the meat filling.
   - In a large skillet or frying pan, heat some olive oil over medium heat.
   - Add the chopped onion and cook until softened and translucent, about 5 minutes.
   - Add the minced garlic and cook for another minute until fragrant.
   - Add the ground meat to the skillet, breaking it up with a spoon. Cook until browned and cooked through.
   - Stir in the chopped tomatoes, tomato paste, ground cinnamon, ground nutmeg, salt, and pepper. Cook for another 5 minutes, allowing the flavors to meld together.
   - Remove from heat and stir in the chopped parsley. If the filling seems too loose, you can add breadcrumbs to bind it slightly.
3. **Make the Béchamel Sauce:**
   - In a medium saucepan, melt the butter over medium heat.
   - Add the flour and whisk constantly for 1-2 minutes to make a roux.
   - Gradually add the warmed milk to the roux, whisking constantly to avoid lumps.
   - Cook the sauce, stirring constantly, until it thickens and coats the back of a spoon (about 5-7 minutes).
   - Season with salt, pepper, and a pinch of nutmeg.
   - Remove from heat and stir in the grated Parmesan cheese until melted and smooth. Set aside.
4. **Assemble and Bake Papoutsakia:**
   - Preheat your oven to 180°C (350°F).
   - Scoop out some of the flesh from each baked eggplant half, leaving a shell about 1 cm thick.
   - Spoon the meat filling into the hollowed-out eggplant halves, dividing it evenly among them.
   - Spoon a generous amount of béchamel sauce over each stuffed eggplant half, covering the meat filling completely.
   - Place the stuffed eggplants back on the baking sheet and bake in the preheated oven for 25-30 minutes, or until the béchamel sauce is golden and bubbly.
5. **Serve:**
   - Remove from the oven and let Papoutsakia cool slightly before serving.
   - Serve warm, garnished with additional chopped parsley if desired.

Tips:

- You can adjust the seasonings and spices in both the meat filling and béchamel sauce according to your taste preferences.
- Papoutsakia can be served as a main dish with a side salad or crusty bread. It's also a great dish to prepare ahead of time and reheat before serving.
- Leftovers can be stored in an airtight container in the refrigerator for a few days. Reheat gently in the oven or microwave before serving.

Enjoy this comforting and flavorful Greek dish of Papoutsakia, featuring tender baked eggplants stuffed with a delicious meat filling and topped with creamy béchamel sauce!

Garides Saganaki (Shrimp in Tomato Sauce)

Ingredients:

- 500g (about 1 lb) large shrimp, peeled and deveined
- 2 tbsp olive oil
- 1 onion, finely chopped
- 3 cloves garlic, minced
- 1 red bell pepper, diced
- 1 yellow bell pepper, diced
- 1 can (400g or 14 oz) diced tomatoes
- 1/4 cup tomato paste
- 1/2 cup dry white wine (optional)
- 1 tsp dried oregano
- 1/2 tsp dried thyme
- Salt and pepper, to taste
- 200g (about 7 oz) feta cheese, crumbled
- Fresh parsley, chopped, for garnish
- Crusty bread, for serving

Instructions:

1. **Prepare the Shrimp:**
   - If the shrimp are not already peeled and deveined, peel them and remove the veins.
   - Pat dry the shrimp with paper towels and season with salt and pepper.
2. **Cook the Sauce:**
   - In a large skillet or frying pan, heat the olive oil over medium heat.
   - Add the chopped onion and cook until softened and translucent, about 5 minutes.
   - Add the minced garlic and cook for another minute until fragrant.
   - Add the diced red and yellow bell peppers to the skillet. Cook for 3-4 minutes until they start to soften.
3. **Add Tomatoes and Seasonings:**
   - Stir in the diced tomatoes, tomato paste, dried oregano, dried thyme, salt, and pepper. If using, pour in the dry white wine.
   - Bring the sauce to a simmer and cook for about 10-15 minutes, stirring occasionally, until the sauce has thickened slightly.
4. **Cook the Shrimp:**
   - Add the seasoned shrimp to the skillet, stirring gently to coat them with the sauce.
   - Cook for 5-7 minutes, or until the shrimp are pink and cooked through. Be careful not to overcook the shrimp, as they can become tough.
5. **Add Feta Cheese:**

- Sprinkle the crumbled feta cheese evenly over the shrimp and sauce in the skillet.
- Cover the skillet and let it simmer for another 2-3 minutes, allowing the cheese to melt slightly.

6. **Serve:**
   - Remove from heat and garnish with chopped fresh parsley.
   - Serve Garides Saganaki hot, straight from the skillet, with crusty bread for dipping into the flavorful tomato and feta sauce.

Tips:

- Adjust the level of spiciness by adding a pinch of red pepper flakes or a dash of hot sauce if desired.
- Make sure the shrimp are evenly sized to ensure even cooking.
- Garides Saganaki is best enjoyed immediately while the shrimp are still tender and the sauce is hot and flavorful.

Enjoy this delicious Garides Saganaki as a delightful Mediterranean dish that combines the freshness of shrimp with the rich flavors of tomato and feta cheese!

Strapatsada (Scrambled Eggs with Tomato and Feta)

Ingredients:

- 4 large eggs
- 2 tbsp olive oil
- 1 small onion, finely chopped
- 2-3 tomatoes, diced (about 1 cup)
- 50g (about 2 oz) feta cheese, crumbled
- 1 tbsp chopped fresh parsley (optional, for garnish)
- Salt and pepper, to taste
- Pinch of dried oregano (optional)
- Crusty bread or pita, for serving

Instructions:

1. **Prepare the Ingredients:**
   - Crack the eggs into a bowl and whisk them together. Season with a pinch of salt and pepper.
2. **Cook the Onions and Tomatoes:**
   - Heat the olive oil in a large skillet or frying pan over medium heat.
   - Add the chopped onion and sauté until softened and translucent, about 3-4 minutes.
3. **Add the Tomatoes:**
   - Add the diced tomatoes to the skillet. Cook for another 5-7 minutes, stirring occasionally, until the tomatoes begin to break down and release their juices.
4. **Scramble the Eggs:**
   - Pour the whisked eggs into the skillet with the tomatoes and onions.
   - Stir gently with a spatula, scraping the bottom of the skillet occasionally, until the eggs are cooked to your desired consistency. The eggs should be creamy and just set.
5. **Add the Feta Cheese:**
   - Crumble the feta cheese over the scrambled eggs. Stir gently to incorporate the cheese into the eggs and tomatoes. The heat of the eggs will melt the feta slightly.
6. **Season and Serve:**
   - Season the Strapatsada with additional salt and pepper to taste.
   - If using, sprinkle chopped fresh parsley and a pinch of dried oregano over the top for added flavor.
7. **Serve Warm:**
   - Serve the Strapatsada immediately, while hot, with crusty bread or pita on the side.

Tips:

- You can customize Strapatsada by adding other ingredients such as bell peppers, spinach, or herbs like basil or dill.
- Adjust the amount of feta cheese according to your preference for richness and saltiness.
- Serve Strapatsada as a standalone dish or alongside a Greek salad for a complete meal.

Enjoy this comforting and flavorful Greek dish of Strapatsada, perfect for a leisurely breakfast or a quick and tasty meal!

Tyropita (Cheese Pie)

Ingredients:

For the Cheese Filling:

- 500g (about 1 lb) feta cheese, crumbled
- 250g (about 9 oz) ricotta cheese or cottage cheese
- 3 large eggs
- 1/4 cup finely chopped fresh parsley
- 1/4 cup finely chopped fresh dill (optional)
- Freshly ground black pepper, to taste

For the Phyllo Dough and Assembly:

- 1 package (about 400g) phyllo dough, thawed if frozen
- 1 cup unsalted butter, melted

Instructions:

1. **Prepare the Cheese Filling:**
    - In a large mixing bowl, combine the crumbled feta cheese, ricotta or cottage cheese, eggs, chopped parsley, chopped dill (if using), and black pepper. Mix well until all ingredients are evenly incorporated. Set aside.
2. **Assemble the Tyropita:**
    - Preheat your oven to 180°C (350°F). Grease a baking dish (about 9x13 inches) with butter.
    - Unwrap the phyllo dough and place it on a clean work surface. Cover it with a damp kitchen towel to prevent it from drying out.
    - Carefully lay one sheet of phyllo dough in the greased baking dish. Brush it lightly with melted butter. Repeat this process, layering and buttering each sheet of phyllo dough, until you have used about half of the package.
3. **Add the Cheese Filling:**
    - Spread the prepared cheese filling evenly over the layered phyllo dough in the baking dish.
4. **Continue Layering:**
    - Continue layering the remaining sheets of phyllo dough on top of the cheese filling, brushing each sheet with melted butter. Fold any excess phyllo dough from the sides over the top layers.
    - Brush the top layer generously with melted butter.
5. **Bake the Tyropita:**
    - Using a sharp knife, score the top layer of phyllo dough into squares or diamond shapes (this will make it easier to cut after baking).
    - Bake in the preheated oven for about 45-50 minutes, or until the Tyropita is golden brown and crispy on top.

6. **Serve:**
    - Remove from the oven and let it cool slightly.
    - Cut into squares or slices along the scored lines.
    - Serve Tyropita warm or at room temperature as a delicious appetizer or snack.

Tips:

- Phyllo dough can dry out quickly, so cover it with a damp kitchen towel while working with it to prevent it from becoming brittle.
- Tyropita can be made ahead of time and reheated in the oven before serving to restore its crispiness.
- Experiment with different herbs and cheeses to customize the filling according to your taste preferences.

Enjoy this classic Greek Tyropita with its layers of flaky phyllo dough and rich cheese filling—a delightful addition to any meal or gathering!

Kolokithokeftedes (Zucchini Fritters)

Ingredients:

- 2 medium zucchinis (about 500g or 1 lb), grated
- 1/2 tsp salt
- 1/2 cup finely chopped green onions (about 2-3 green onions)
- 1/4 cup finely chopped fresh dill
- 1/4 cup finely chopped fresh mint (optional)
- 1/2 cup crumbled feta cheese
- 2 large eggs, lightly beaten
- 1/2 cup all-purpose flour
- 1/2 tsp baking powder
- Freshly ground black pepper, to taste
- Olive oil, for frying

Instructions:

1. **Prepare the Zucchini:**
   - Grate the zucchinis using a box grater or a food processor fitted with a grating attachment. Place the grated zucchini in a colander and sprinkle with salt. Let it sit for about 10-15 minutes to allow excess moisture to drain.
2. **Squeeze out Excess Moisture:**
   - After draining, squeeze handfuls of the grated zucchini tightly to remove as much moisture as possible. Transfer the squeezed zucchini to a clean bowl.
3. **Combine Ingredients:**
   - To the bowl with the grated zucchini, add the chopped green onions, fresh dill, fresh mint (if using), crumbled feta cheese, and lightly beaten eggs. Mix well to combine.
4. **Add Flour and Baking Powder:**
   - Sprinkle the flour and baking powder over the zucchini mixture. Season with freshly ground black pepper to taste. Mix until all ingredients are evenly incorporated and a sticky batter forms.
5. **Fry the Kolokithokeftedes:**
   - Heat a generous amount of olive oil in a large skillet or frying pan over medium heat.
   - Using a spoon or your hands, scoop out portions of the zucchini mixture and shape them into small patties or fritters, about 2-3 inches in diameter and 1/2 inch thick.
   - Carefully place the fritters into the hot oil, working in batches to avoid overcrowding the pan. Fry for about 3-4 minutes on each side, or until golden brown and crispy.

- Remove the fritters from the skillet and place them on a plate lined with paper towels to absorb any excess oil. Repeat until all the batter is used, adding more olive oil to the pan as needed between batches.

6. **Serve:**
   - Serve the Kolokithokeftedes warm, garnished with additional chopped fresh herbs if desired.
   - Serve with tzatziki sauce, yogurt dip, or a squeeze of lemon juice on the side for dipping.

Tips:

- Ensure the grated zucchini is well drained before mixing it with the other ingredients to prevent the fritters from becoming soggy.
- You can adjust the herbs and seasonings in the fritters according to your taste preferences. Fresh parsley or basil can also be added for additional flavor.
- Leftover Kolokithokeftedes can be stored in an airtight container in the refrigerator for a few days. Reheat in the oven or toaster oven to maintain their crispiness.

Enjoy these crispy and flavorful Kolokithokeftedes as a delightful appetizer or side dish, perfect for showcasing the fresh flavors of zucchini and herbs in Greek cuisine!

Pitarakia (Sweet Fried Dough)

Ingredients:

For the Dough:

- 3 cups all-purpose flour
- 1/2 tsp baking powder
- Pinch of salt
- 1/4 cup granulated sugar
- 1/2 cup unsalted butter, melted
- 1/2 cup milk
- 1 large egg
- Zest of 1 lemon
- Vegetable oil, for frying

For the Syrup:

- 1 cup honey
- 1 cup water
- 1 cinnamon stick (optional)
- Zest of 1 lemon

For Serving (Optional):

- Chopped walnuts or sesame seeds (for garnish)

Instructions:

1. **Make the Dough:**
   - In a large bowl, sift together the flour, baking powder, and salt.
   - In a separate bowl, whisk together the melted butter and sugar until smooth. Add the egg, milk, and lemon zest, and whisk until well combined.
   - Gradually add the wet ingredients to the dry ingredients, stirring with a spoon or your hands, until a soft dough forms. If the dough is too sticky, add a little more flour.
2. **Shape the Pitarakia:**
   - Divide the dough into small portions and roll each portion into a ball (about the size of a walnut). Flatten each ball slightly with your palms to form small discs or oval shapes.
3. **Fry the Pitarakia:**
   - In a deep skillet or frying pan, heat vegetable oil over medium heat until it reaches 170-180°C (340-360°F), or until a small piece of dough sizzles immediately when dropped in.

- Carefully place a few pieces of dough into the hot oil, being careful not to overcrowd the pan. Fry for about 2-3 minutes on each side, or until golden brown and crispy.
- Use a slotted spoon to remove the fried Pitarakia from the oil and place them on a plate lined with paper towels to drain excess oil. Repeat with the remaining dough.

4. **Make the Syrup:**
   - In a saucepan, combine the honey, water, cinnamon stick (if using), and lemon zest. Bring to a boil over medium-high heat, stirring occasionally.
   - Reduce the heat and simmer for about 5-7 minutes, or until the syrup slightly thickens and coats the back of a spoon.
   - Remove from heat and discard the cinnamon stick and lemon zest.

5. **Soak the Pitarakia:**
   - While the syrup is still warm, carefully dip each fried Pitaraki into the syrup, coating it thoroughly. Let it soak for a few seconds to absorb the syrup.

6. **Serve:**
   - Transfer the soaked Pitarakia to a serving platter. Optionally, sprinkle chopped walnuts or sesame seeds over the top for added texture and flavor.
   - Serve Pitarakia warm or at room temperature. They are best enjoyed fresh on the day they are made.

Tips:

- Ensure the oil is hot enough before frying to achieve crispy and evenly browned Pitarakia.
- You can adjust the sweetness of the syrup by adding more or less honey according to your preference.
- Pitarakia can be stored in an airtight container at room temperature for a day or two. Reheat briefly in the oven before serving to refresh their crispiness.

Enjoy these delicious Greek Pitarakia, with their crispy exterior and sticky sweetness from the honey syrup—a perfect treat for special occasions or as a delightful dessert!

Marides Tiganites (Fried Anchovies)

Ingredients:

- Fresh anchovies (about 500g or 1 lb), cleaned and gutted
- All-purpose flour, for dredging
- Salt and pepper, to taste
- Vegetable oil, for frying
- Lemon wedges, for serving

Instructions:

1. **Prepare the Anchovies:**
    - Rinse the anchovies under cold water and pat them dry with paper towels.
    - If the anchovies are large, you can cut off the heads and trim the tails, but leaving them whole is traditional.
2. **Dredge the Anchovies:**
    - Season the all-purpose flour with salt and pepper on a plate.
    - Lightly dredge each anchovy in the seasoned flour, shaking off any excess.
3. **Fry the Anchovies:**
    - In a deep skillet or frying pan, heat enough vegetable oil to cover the anchovies over medium-high heat until it reaches 180°C (350°F).
    - Carefully place a few anchovies at a time into the hot oil. Be cautious not to overcrowd the pan to ensure even frying.
    - Fry the anchovies for about 2-3 minutes on each side, or until they are golden brown and crispy.
    - Use a slotted spoon to remove the fried anchovies from the oil and place them on a plate lined with paper towels to drain excess oil. Repeat with the remaining anchovies.
4. **Serve:**
    - Arrange the fried anchovies on a serving platter.
    - Serve hot, garnished with lemon wedges for squeezing over the anchovies.

Tips:

- Fresh anchovies are preferred for this dish, as they have a delicate flavor and fry up beautifully.
- Make sure the oil is hot enough before frying to achieve crispy anchovies.
- You can season the flour with additional spices like paprika or dried herbs for extra flavor if desired.

Enjoy these crispy and delicious Marides Tiganites as a delightful appetizer or main dish, perfect for sharing Mediterranean flavors with friends and family!

Dakos (Barley Rusk Salad)

Ingredients:

- Barley rusk (paximadi) or whole grain rusk (can substitute with whole grain crackers or toasted bread)
- Ripe tomatoes, thinly sliced or chopped
- Feta cheese, crumbled
- Kalamata olives, pitted and chopped
- Capers, drained
- Red onion, thinly sliced (optional)
- Fresh oregano or dried oregano
- Extra virgin olive oil
- Red wine vinegar (optional)
- Salt and pepper, to taste

Instructions:

1. **Prepare the Barley Rusk:**
    - If using barley rusk (paximadi), soak it briefly in water to soften slightly, then let it drain. This step helps to soften the hard rusk.
2. **Assemble the Dakos:**
    - Place the softened barley rusk or whole grain rusk on serving plates or a platter.
    - Top each piece of rusk generously with sliced or chopped tomatoes.
    - Sprinkle crumbled feta cheese over the tomatoes.
    - Scatter chopped Kalamata olives and capers over the cheese and tomatoes.
    - If using, add thinly sliced red onion for an extra layer of flavor.
3. **Season and Dress:**
    - Drizzle extra virgin olive oil generously over each serving.
    - Optionally, sprinkle a splash of red wine vinegar over the salads for a tangy kick (this is traditional but optional).
    - Season with salt and freshly ground black pepper to taste.
    - Garnish with fresh oregano leaves or sprinkle dried oregano over the top for added flavor.
4. **Serve:**
    - Serve Dakos immediately, allowing the rusk to absorb the flavors of the tomatoes, cheese, and olives.
    - Enjoy Dakos as a refreshing salad or appetizer, perfect for a Mediterranean-inspired meal.

Tips:

- Barley rusk (paximadi) is traditionally used in Dakos for its hearty texture, but you can use whole grain rusk or even toasted whole grain bread as a substitute.

- Adjust the toppings according to your taste preferences. You can add cucumber slices, bell peppers, or even anchovies for additional flavor.
- Dakos is best enjoyed fresh, but you can prepare the components ahead of time and assemble just before serving to maintain the crisp texture of the rusk.

Enjoy this traditional Cretan dish of Dakos, showcasing the vibrant flavors of the Mediterranean with ripe tomatoes, tangy feta cheese, and briny olives!

Pitaroudia (Chickpea Fritters)

Ingredients:

- 2 cups dried chickpeas, soaked overnight (or use canned chickpeas, drained and rinsed)
- 1 medium onion, finely chopped
- 3 garlic cloves, minced
- 1/2 cup chopped fresh parsley
- 1/4 cup chopped fresh dill
- 1 tsp ground cumin
- 1 tsp ground coriander
- 1/2 tsp smoked paprika (optional)
- Salt and pepper, to taste
- 1/2 cup all-purpose flour
- Vegetable oil, for frying

Instructions:

1. **Prepare the Chickpeas:**
    - If using dried chickpeas, drain and rinse them after soaking overnight. If using canned chickpeas, drain and rinse them well.
2. **Make the Chickpea Mixture:**
    - In a food processor, pulse the chickpeas until coarsely chopped. You want some texture, so avoid over-processing into a paste.
    - Transfer the chopped chickpeas to a large mixing bowl. Add the finely chopped onion, minced garlic, chopped parsley, chopped dill, ground cumin, ground coriander, smoked paprika (if using), salt, and pepper. Mix well to combine.
3. **Form the Pitaroudia:**
    - Gradually add the all-purpose flour to the chickpea mixture, stirring until well combined. The flour helps bind the mixture together.
    - Take a portion of the mixture and shape it into small patties or fritters, about 2-3 inches in diameter and 1/2 inch thick. Repeat with the remaining mixture.
4. **Fry the Pitaroudia:**
    - In a large skillet or frying pan, heat vegetable oil over medium-high heat until it reaches 180°C (350°F).
    - Carefully place a few Pitaroudia into the hot oil, being careful not to overcrowd the pan. Fry for about 3-4 minutes on each side, or until golden brown and crispy.
    - Use a slotted spoon to remove the fried Pitaroudia from the oil and place them on a plate lined with paper towels to drain excess oil. Repeat with the remaining mixture.
5. **Serve:**
    - Serve Pitaroudia warm as a meze or appetizer.
    - Optionally, serve with tzatziki sauce, yogurt dip, or a squeeze of lemon juice on the side for dipping.

Tips:

- Adjust the seasoning and herbs according to your taste preferences. You can add more spices or herbs like mint for variation.
- For a healthier option, you can bake the Pitaroudia in the oven instead of frying. Preheat the oven to 200°C (400°F) and bake for about 15-20 minutes, flipping halfway through, until golden brown and crispy.
- Pitaroudia can be stored in an airtight container in the refrigerator for a few days. Reheat in the oven or toaster oven to restore their crispiness before serving.

Enjoy these flavorful Greek chickpea fritters, Pitaroudia, as a delicious appetizer or side dish, perfect for sharing with family and friends!

Soutzoukakia (Meatballs in Tomato Sauce)

Ingredients:

For the Meatballs (Soutzoukakia):

- 500g (about 1 lb) ground beef or lamb (or a mixture of both)
- 1/2 cup breadcrumbs
- 1 small onion, grated
- 2 cloves garlic, minced
- 1 egg
- 1/4 cup chopped fresh parsley
- 1/2 tsp ground cumin
- 1/2 tsp ground coriander
- 1/2 tsp dried oregano
- Salt and pepper, to taste
- All-purpose flour, for dredging
- Olive oil, for frying

For the Tomato Sauce:

- 1 can (400g or 14 oz) crushed tomatoes
- 1/2 cup tomato paste
- 1 cup beef or vegetable broth
- 2 cloves garlic, minced
- 1/2 tsp dried oregano
- 1/2 tsp paprika
- Salt and pepper, to taste
- Fresh parsley, chopped, for garnish

Instructions:

1. **Make the Meatballs (Soutzoukakia):**
   - In a large mixing bowl, combine the ground beef (or lamb), breadcrumbs, grated onion, minced garlic, egg, chopped parsley, ground cumin, ground coriander, dried oregano, salt, and pepper. Mix until well combined.
   - Shape the mixture into elongated meatballs, about 2 inches long and 1 inch thick.
   - Roll each meatball in flour to lightly coat, shaking off any excess.
2. **Fry the Meatballs:**
   - In a large skillet or frying pan, heat olive oil over medium-high heat.
   - Add the meatballs in batches, making sure not to overcrowd the pan. Fry them for about 3-4 minutes on each side, or until they are browned and cooked through. Transfer the meatballs to a plate lined with paper towels to drain excess oil. Set aside.
3. **Prepare the Tomato Sauce:**

- In the same skillet (or a separate saucepan), add a bit more olive oil if needed. Saute the minced garlic for about 1 minute until fragrant.
- Add the crushed tomatoes, tomato paste, beef or vegetable broth, dried oregano, paprika, salt, and pepper. Stir well to combine.
- Bring the sauce to a simmer over medium heat. Reduce the heat to low and let it simmer gently for about 10-15 minutes, stirring occasionally, to allow the flavors to meld and the sauce to thicken slightly.

4. **Simmer the Meatballs in the Sauce:**
   - Carefully add the fried meatballs back into the skillet with the tomato sauce. Spoon some of the sauce over the meatballs to coat them.
   - Cover the skillet with a lid and let the meatballs simmer in the sauce for another 10-15 minutes, allowing them to absorb the flavors of the sauce.
5. **Serve:**
   - Remove from heat and garnish with chopped fresh parsley.
   - Serve Soutzoukakia hot, accompanied by rice, potatoes, or crusty bread for soaking up the delicious tomato sauce.

Tips:

- You can adjust the spices and seasoning in both the meatballs and the tomato sauce according to your taste preference. Some variations include adding cinnamon or allspice for a hint of sweetness.
- For a richer sauce, you can add a splash of red wine or a tablespoon of Worcestershire sauce.
- Soutzoukakia can be made ahead of time and stored in the refrigerator for a day or two. Reheat gently on the stove before serving to ensure the meatballs stay tender and flavorful.

Enjoy these hearty and flavorful Greek meatballs, Soutzoukakia, as a comforting and satisfying meal that showcases the vibrant flavors of the Mediterranean!

Lazarakia (Lenten Cookies)

Ingredients:

- 3 cups all-purpose flour
- 1 cup sugar
- 1/2 cup orange juice
- 1/2 cup olive oil
- Zest of 1 orange
- Zest of 1 lemon
- 1 tsp ground cloves
- 1 tsp ground cinnamon
- 1/2 tsp ground nutmeg
- 1/2 tsp baking soda
- 1/2 tsp baking powder
- Pinch of salt
- Whole cloves, for decoration

Instructions:

1. **Preheat the Oven:**
   - Preheat your oven to 180°C (350°F). Line a baking sheet with parchment paper.
2. **Prepare the Dough:**
   - In a large mixing bowl, whisk together the flour, sugar, ground cloves, ground cinnamon, ground nutmeg, baking soda, baking powder, and salt.
   - Add the olive oil, orange juice, orange zest, and lemon zest to the dry ingredients. Mix until a dough forms. If the dough is too sticky, you can add a bit more flour, one tablespoon at a time, until it comes together and is easy to handle.
3. **Shape the Cookies:**
   - Take portions of the dough and shape them into small round or oval cookies, about 1.5 inches in diameter. Place them on the prepared baking sheet, leaving a little space between each cookie.
4. **Decorate with Cloves:**
   - Press one whole clove into the center of each cookie. This is a traditional decoration and also infuses a subtle flavor into the cookies.
5. **Bake the Cookies:**
   - Bake in the preheated oven for 20-25 minutes, or until the cookies are lightly golden brown on the bottom. The tops of the cookies should remain pale.
6. **Cool and Serve:**
   - Remove from the oven and let the cookies cool on the baking sheet for a few minutes.
   - Transfer the cookies to a wire rack to cool completely before serving.
7. **Optional Glaze (if desired):**

- You can optionally brush the cooled cookies with a simple glaze made from powdered sugar and a little orange juice for added sweetness and shine.
8. **Serve and Enjoy:**
    - Serve Lazarakia cookies with a cup of Greek coffee or tea. They are traditionally enjoyed during Holy Week but can be savored any time as a delightful treat.

Tips:

- The amount of flour needed may vary slightly depending on factors like humidity, so adjust accordingly to achieve a smooth dough.
- These cookies are traditionally not overly sweet. If you prefer sweeter cookies, you can increase the amount of sugar in the recipe.
- Store Lazarakia cookies in an airtight container at room temperature. They can last for several days, although they are best enjoyed fresh.

Enjoy making and sharing these traditional Greek Lenten cookies, Lazarakia, as a delicious and symbolic treat during the Easter season!

Anginares a la Polita (Artichokes with Lemon and Olive Oil)

Ingredients:

- 6-8 medium artichokes
- Juice of 2-3 lemons
- 1/2 cup extra virgin olive oil
- 1 onion, finely chopped
- 3-4 spring onions, finely chopped
- 2 carrots, peeled and sliced
- 1 celery stalk, sliced
- 1/2 cup chopped fresh dill
- 1/2 cup chopped fresh parsley
- 1-2 potatoes, peeled and sliced (optional, for thickening the sauce)
- Salt and freshly ground black pepper, to taste
- Water or vegetable broth, as needed

Instructions:

1. **Prepare the Artichokes:**
   - Fill a large bowl with water and squeeze the juice of 1 lemon into it.
   - Trim the tough outer leaves of the artichokes. Cut off the top third of each artichoke and trim the stem, leaving about 2 inches attached.
   - Rub the cut surfaces with the remaining lemon halves to prevent discoloration. Place the trimmed artichokes in the bowl of lemon water.
2. **Cook the Vegetables:**
   - In a large, deep skillet or pot, heat the olive oil over medium heat. Add the chopped onion and spring onions. Sauté for 3-4 minutes until softened.
   - Add the sliced carrots and celery. Cook for another 5 minutes until they begin to soften.
3. **Prepare the Sauce:**
   - Drain the artichokes from the lemon water and add them to the pot with the vegetables.
   - Pour in the juice of the remaining lemons.
   - Add chopped dill, parsley, salt, and pepper to taste. Stir to combine.
   - If using potatoes for thickening, layer them on top of the artichokes and vegetables.
4. **Cook the Dish:**
   - Add enough water or vegetable broth to almost cover the artichokes and vegetables.
   - Bring the mixture to a boil, then reduce the heat to low. Cover the pot and simmer gently for 45-60 minutes, or until the artichokes and vegetables are tender.
   - Check occasionally and add more liquid if needed to maintain a sauce-like consistency.

5. **Serve:**
    - Once cooked, remove from heat and let it cool slightly.
    - Serve Anginares a la Polita warm or at room temperature, garnished with additional fresh herbs if desired.

Tips:

- If fresh artichokes are not available, you can use frozen or canned artichoke hearts. Adjust cooking time accordingly.
- Anginares a la Polita can be served as a main dish with crusty bread or as a side dish alongside grilled fish or chicken.
- Leftovers can be refrigerated in an airtight container for a few days. Reheat gently on the stove or in the microwave before serving.

Enjoy the fresh and delicate flavors of Anginares a la Polita, a classic Greek dish that celebrates the simplicity and goodness of artichokes cooked in olive oil and lemon!

Pasteli (Sesame Seed and Honey Bars)

Ingredients:

- 1 cup sesame seeds (white or a mixture of white and black)
- 1/2 cup honey (preferably Greek honey for authentic flavor)

Instructions:

1. **Toast the Sesame Seeds:**
    - Heat a dry skillet or frying pan over medium heat. Add the sesame seeds and toast them, stirring frequently, until they are golden brown and fragrant. This usually takes about 3-5 minutes. Be careful not to burn them. Transfer the toasted sesame seeds to a plate and let them cool slightly.
2. **Prepare the Honey Mixture:**
    - In a medium saucepan, heat the honey over medium-low heat until it becomes thin and runny. This makes it easier to mix with the sesame seeds.
3. **Combine Sesame Seeds and Honey:**
    - Add the toasted sesame seeds to the warm honey in the saucepan. Stir well to coat the sesame seeds evenly with the honey. Continue stirring over low heat for a few minutes until the mixture thickens slightly and starts to pull away from the sides of the pan.
4. **Shape the Pasteli:**
    - While the mixture is still warm, transfer it onto a sheet of parchment paper or a silicone mat. Place another sheet of parchment paper on top.
    - Use a rolling pin to flatten and spread out the mixture evenly to your desired thickness, typically about 1/4 to 1/2 inch thick.
5. **Cut Into Bars:**
    - While the mixture is still warm and pliable, use a sharp knife to cut it into rectangular or diamond-shaped bars. You can also use cookie cutters for different shapes if preferred.
6. **Let it Cool:**
    - Allow the Pasteli bars to cool completely at room temperature. As they cool, they will firm up and become more solid.
7. **Store and Serve:**
    - Once completely cooled and firm, transfer the Pasteli bars to an airtight container with layers of parchment paper between them to prevent sticking.
    - Pasteli can be stored at room temperature for several weeks. In warm climates, it's best to store them in the refrigerator to keep them firm.

Tips:

- You can customize Pasteli by adding a pinch of sea salt or a dash of cinnamon for extra flavor.

- Be cautious when heating the honey, as it can easily burn. Keep the heat low and stir constantly.
- Use high-quality honey for the best flavor. Greek thyme honey is particularly delicious if you can find it.

Enjoy these homemade Greek sesame seed and honey bars, Pasteli, as a nutritious snack or dessert that showcases the simplicity and deliciousness of Mediterranean ingredients!

Imam Baildi (Stuffed Eggplant)

Ingredients:

- 4 small to medium-sized eggplants
- 1/2 cup olive oil, divided
- 1 large onion, finely chopped
- 3-4 garlic cloves, minced
- 2 large tomatoes, grated (or 1 can (400g) crushed tomatoes)
- 1 tbsp tomato paste
- 1 tsp sugar
- 1/2 cup chopped fresh parsley
- Salt and pepper, to taste

Instructions:

1. **Prepare the Eggplants:**
    - Wash the eggplants and pat them dry. Cut each eggplant in half lengthwise.
    - Score the flesh of each eggplant half in a crisscross pattern, being careful not to cut through the skin. This helps the eggplants cook evenly and absorb more flavor.
2. **Sauté the Eggplants:**
    - In a large skillet or frying pan, heat 1/4 cup of olive oil over medium-high heat.
    - Place the eggplant halves in the skillet, cut side down. Cook for about 5 minutes, or until they are golden brown. Turn them over and cook for another 3-4 minutes on the other side. Remove the eggplants from the skillet and set them aside.
3. **Prepare the Tomato Sauce:**
    - In the same skillet, add the remaining 1/4 cup of olive oil.
    - Add the finely chopped onion and sauté until softened and translucent, about 5-7 minutes.
    - Add the minced garlic and cook for another 1-2 minutes until fragrant.
    - Stir in the grated tomatoes (or crushed tomatoes), tomato paste, sugar, chopped parsley, salt, and pepper. Mix well to combine.
4. **Assemble and Cook:**
    - Place the eggplant halves back into the skillet, cut side up, nestled into the tomato sauce.
    - Spoon some of the tomato mixture over each eggplant half to coat them generously.
    - Cover the skillet with a lid and simmer over low heat for 30-40 minutes, or until the eggplants are very tender and the sauce has thickened. Occasionally spoon some of the sauce over the eggplants to keep them moist.
5. **Serve:**
    - Once cooked, remove from heat and let it cool slightly.

- Serve Imam Baildi warm or at room temperature, garnished with additional chopped parsley if desired.

Tips:

- Choose small to medium-sized eggplants for Imam Baildi, as they tend to be more tender and flavorful.
- Adjust the seasoning according to your taste preference. You can add a pinch of red pepper flakes for a hint of spice.
- Imam Baildi is often served as a vegetarian main dish or as a side dish to accompany grilled meats or fish.
- Leftovers can be stored in an airtight container in the refrigerator for up to 3 days. Reheat gently on the stove before serving.

Enjoy this classic Greek dish of Imam Baildi, where tender eggplants soak up the flavors of the rich tomato sauce, creating a comforting and satisfying meal!

Karithopita (Walnut Cake)

Ingredients:

For the Cake:

- 1 cup walnuts, finely chopped
- 1 cup all-purpose flour
- 1 tsp baking powder
- 1/2 tsp baking soda
- 1/2 tsp ground cinnamon
- 1/4 tsp ground cloves
- 1/4 tsp ground nutmeg
- Pinch of salt
- 3 large eggs, at room temperature
- 1 cup granulated sugar
- 1/2 cup Greek yogurt or sour cream
- 1/2 cup olive oil
- Zest of 1 orange
- Zest of 1 lemon
- 1/4 cup orange juice
- 1/4 cup brandy or cognac (optional)

For the Syrup:

- 1 cup water
- 1 cup granulated sugar
- Zest of 1 lemon
- Zest of 1 orange
- 1 cinnamon stick (optional)
- 1/4 cup honey (optional, for a richer syrup)

Instructions:

1. **Prepare the Cake:**
    - Preheat your oven to 180°C (350°F). Grease and flour a 9-inch round cake pan or line it with parchment paper.
2. **Toast and Prepare the Walnuts:**
    - Spread the chopped walnuts on a baking sheet and toast them in the preheated oven for about 5-7 minutes, or until lightly golden and fragrant. Remove from the oven and let them cool.
3. **Mix the Dry Ingredients:**
    - In a bowl, whisk together the flour, baking powder, baking soda, ground cinnamon, ground cloves, ground nutmeg, and salt. Set aside.
4. **Prepare the Batter:**

- In a large mixing bowl, beat the eggs and sugar together until pale and creamy.
- Add the Greek yogurt (or sour cream), olive oil, orange zest, lemon zest, orange juice, and brandy (if using). Mix until well combined.

5. **Combine Dry and Wet Ingredients:**
   - Gradually add the dry ingredients to the wet ingredients, mixing until just combined.
   - Fold in the toasted walnuts until evenly distributed throughout the batter.

6. **Bake the Cake:**
   - Pour the batter into the prepared cake pan and smooth the top with a spatula.
   - Bake in the preheated oven for 35-40 minutes, or until a toothpick inserted into the center comes out clean.

7. **Prepare the Syrup:**
   - While the cake is baking, prepare the syrup. In a saucepan, combine the water, sugar, lemon zest, orange zest, and cinnamon stick (if using).
   - Bring to a boil over medium-high heat, then reduce the heat and simmer for 5-7 minutes, stirring occasionally, until the sugar is completely dissolved and the syrup slightly thickens.
   - Remove from heat and stir in the honey (if using). Let the syrup cool slightly.

8. **Soak the Cake:**
   - Once the cake is baked and while it is still warm, pour the warm syrup evenly over the top of the cake.
   - Allow the cake to absorb the syrup and cool completely in the pan before removing.

9. **Serve:**
   - Once cooled, remove the cake from the pan and slice.
   - Serve Karithopita slices at room temperature, optionally garnished with whipped cream, a sprinkle of powdered sugar, or additional chopped walnuts.

Tips:

- The brandy or cognac in the cake batter adds depth of flavor, but you can omit it if preferred.
- Make sure the cake is warm and the syrup is warm when pouring the syrup over the cake for better absorption.
- Karithopita can be stored in an airtight container at room temperature for a few days. The flavors often develop and improve the day after baking.

Enjoy this delicious Greek Walnut Cake, Karithopita, with its rich flavors of nuts, spices, and citrus, perfect for any occasion or as a sweet ending to a Mediterranean-inspired meal!

Fakes Soupa (Lentil Soup)

Ingredients:

- 1 1/2 cups dried brown or green lentils, rinsed and picked over
- 1 onion, finely chopped
- 2 carrots, diced
- 2 celery stalks, diced
- 3 cloves garlic, minced
- 2 tbsp olive oil
- 1 can (400g or 14 oz) crushed tomatoes
- 1 tbsp tomato paste
- 1 bay leaf
- 1 tsp dried oregano
- 1/2 tsp dried thyme
- 1/2 tsp ground cumin
- 1/2 tsp smoked paprika (optional)
- 6 cups vegetable broth or water
- Salt and freshly ground black pepper, to taste
- Juice of 1 lemon (optional)
- Fresh parsley, chopped, for garnish

Instructions:

1. **Prepare the Lentils:**
   - Rinse the lentils under cold water and remove any debris. Set them aside.
2. **Sauté the Vegetables:**
   - In a large pot or Dutch oven, heat the olive oil over medium heat. Add the chopped onion, carrots, and celery. Sauté for 5-7 minutes, or until the vegetables begin to soften.
3. **Add Garlic and Spices:**
   - Add the minced garlic, bay leaf, dried oregano, dried thyme, ground cumin, and smoked paprika (if using). Cook for 1-2 minutes until fragrant, stirring constantly.
4. **Add Lentils and Tomatoes:**
   - Stir in the rinsed lentils, crushed tomatoes, and tomato paste. Mix well to combine with the vegetables and spices.
5. **Simmer the Soup:**
   - Pour in the vegetable broth or water, ensuring it covers the lentils and vegetables. Bring the mixture to a boil, then reduce the heat to low.
   - Cover and simmer gently for 30-40 minutes, or until the lentils are tender and cooked through. Stir occasionally to prevent sticking, and add more broth or water if needed for desired consistency.
6. **Season and Serve:**

- Once the lentils are cooked to your liking, season the soup with salt and pepper to taste. If desired, stir in the juice of one lemon for a hint of brightness.
- Remove the bay leaf before serving.

7. **Garnish and Serve:**
    - Ladle the Fakes Soupa into bowls. Garnish with chopped fresh parsley.
    - Serve hot, optionally with a drizzle of extra virgin olive oil and crusty bread on the side.

Tips:

- For a creamier texture, you can partially blend the soup with an immersion blender or blend a portion in a regular blender and then mix it back into the pot.
- This soup develops even more flavor the next day, so it's great for leftovers. Store in the refrigerator in an airtight container for up to 4 days.
- Fakes Soupa is traditionally served as a main dish with a side of crusty bread or a simple salad.

Enjoy this comforting and nutritious Greek Lentil Soup, Fakes Soupa, that's full of wholesome ingredients and Mediterranean flavors!

Psomi (Greek Bread)

Ingredients:

- 500g (about 4 cups) bread flour (you can also use all-purpose flour)
- 1 tsp salt
- 1 tsp sugar
- 1 tbsp active dry yeast
- 1 1/4 cups lukewarm water
- Extra flour for dusting

Instructions:

1. **Activate the Yeast:**
   - In a small bowl, combine the lukewarm water, sugar, and yeast. Stir gently and let it sit for about 5-10 minutes until the mixture becomes frothy. This indicates that the yeast is activated.
2. **Mix the Dough:**
   - In a large mixing bowl, combine the bread flour and salt. Make a well in the center and pour in the activated yeast mixture.
   - Use a wooden spoon or your hands to mix the ingredients together until a dough starts to form.
3. **Knead the Dough:**
   - Transfer the dough onto a lightly floured surface. Knead the dough for about 8-10 minutes until it becomes smooth and elastic. Add more flour as needed if the dough is too sticky.
4. **First Rise:**
   - Place the kneaded dough in a lightly oiled bowl, turning the dough to coat it with oil. Cover the bowl with a clean kitchen towel or plastic wrap.
   - Let the dough rise in a warm, draft-free place for about 1-1.5 hours, or until it doubles in size.
5. **Shape the Bread:**
   - Once the dough has risen, punch it down gently to release the air. Transfer it to a lightly floured surface and shape it into a round or oval loaf.
   - Place the shaped loaf on a baking sheet lined with parchment paper. Cover it loosely with a clean kitchen towel and let it rise again for about 30-45 minutes.
6. **Preheat the Oven:**
   - Preheat your oven to 220°C (425°F). Place a shallow baking pan on the bottom rack of the oven.
7. **Score the Bread (Optional):**
   - Using a sharp knife or razor blade, score the top of the bread with a few diagonal slashes. This helps the bread expand while baking.
8. **Bake the Bread:**

- Just before placing the bread in the oven, pour a cup of water into the shallow baking pan on the bottom rack. This creates steam which helps to develop a crusty exterior.
- Place the bread in the preheated oven and bake for 25-30 minutes, or until the bread is golden brown and sounds hollow when tapped on the bottom.

9. **Cool and Serve:**
   - Transfer the bread to a wire rack and let it cool completely before slicing.
   - Serve Psomi (Greek Bread) fresh, with olive oil, dips, or alongside your favorite Mediterranean dishes.

Tips:

- You can add variations to the basic recipe by incorporating herbs like rosemary or thyme into the dough, or adding olives or sun-dried tomatoes for extra flavor.
- Make sure to let the bread cool completely before slicing to allow it to set properly and prevent it from becoming gummy.
- Store leftover Psomi in a paper bag or bread box at room temperature. It's best eaten fresh, but you can toast slices the next day for a delicious treat.

Enjoy making this traditional Greek bread, Psomi, and savor the wonderful aroma and taste of homemade bread that's perfect for any meal!

Loukaniko (Greek Sausage)

Ingredients:

- 1 kg (about 2.2 lbs) ground pork (preferably with some fat)
- 100g (about 3.5 oz) pork fatback, finely chopped (optional, but recommended for moisture)
- 2-3 garlic cloves, minced
- 1 tbsp salt
- 2 tsp ground black pepper
- 2 tsp ground coriander
- 2 tsp ground cumin
- 1 tsp ground fennel seeds
- 1/2 tsp ground cinnamon
- 1/2 tsp ground allspice
- 1/4 tsp ground cloves
- 1/4 cup red wine vinegar
- 1/4 cup dry red wine (optional, for additional flavor)
- Hog casings, soaked in water for at least 30 minutes (available at butcher shops)

Instructions:

1. **Prepare the Casings:**
   - Rinse the hog casings thoroughly under cold water to remove any excess salt. Soak them in warm water for at least 30 minutes to soften them.
2. **Mix the Ingredients:**
   - In a large mixing bowl, combine the ground pork, chopped pork fatback (if using), minced garlic, salt, pepper, coriander, cumin, fennel seeds, cinnamon, allspice, and cloves.
   - Add the red wine vinegar and red wine (if using). Mix well until all the ingredients are evenly incorporated and the mixture becomes somewhat sticky.
3. **Stuff the Casings:**
   - Attach a sausage stuffer attachment to a stand mixer or use a sausage stuffer if available.
   - Carefully slide the soaked hog casings onto the sausage stuffer tube, leaving a small overhang at the end to tie off later.
   - Stuff the sausage mixture into the casings, ensuring they are evenly filled but not overstuffed to avoid bursting. Twist or tie off the sausages at desired intervals to form links.
4. **Let the Sausages Rest:**
   - Once all the sausages are stuffed and tied, prick any air bubbles with a needle and gently squeeze out any excess air.
   - Let the sausages rest in the refrigerator for at least 2 hours or overnight to allow the flavors to meld.

5. **Cook or Store:**
   - Loukaniko can be grilled, pan-fried, or baked in the oven until fully cooked through. Cook until the internal temperature reaches 160°F (71°C).
   - Alternatively, you can freeze the sausages (uncooked or cooked) for later use. Store them in an airtight container or freezer bags.
6. **Serve:**
   - Once cooked, serve Loukaniko hot off the grill or pan-fried, alongside fresh bread, tzatziki, or your favorite Greek sides.

Tips:

- Adjust the spice levels to your preference. You can add more or less of certain spices like garlic, pepper, or cumin.
- If you don't have a sausage stuffer, you can shape the mixture into patties or meatballs instead.
- Loukaniko pairs well with a variety of Mediterranean dishes and is perfect for outdoor grilling or indoor cooking.

Enjoy the flavors of homemade Loukaniko, a delicious Greek sausage that's versatile and full of Mediterranean spices!

www.ingramcontent.com/pod-product-compliance
Lightning Source LLC
LaVergne TN
LVHW081602060526
838201LV00054B/2033